Praise for *The Quintessential Guide to Singing*

"This is one of the most thorough 'How To' books I have ever seen. I do hope it can get to those who so desperately need this kind of coaching and workout."
--- **Carolyn Black Hightower**, educator, choir director.

"A fascinating read. A guide that is in depth and helpful in understanding the voice and how the rest of the body is intricately, and intrinsically, involved in the act of singing. Ms. Gulian has given us something that is both practical and cerebral. It will take your singing to another level."
--- **Marc Teamaker**, singer-songwriter

"Ann Gulian's vocal coaching has given me the confidence and toolbox to perform and teach songs in challenging conditions. The 'Quintessential Guide to Singing' successfully packages her teaching talents as if you were standing in the room with her. Each section includes different exercises to approach the same goal. If one doesn't work for your particular voice, try the next. You'll thank her for the anatomy lessons!"
--- **Laura Copel**, singer, songwriter, educator

"The Quintessential Guide to Singing demystifies and dissects the fundamental components of the voice in a clear, concise, and accessible format. It describes not only the tools needed to build a strong, reliable instrument, but how and why the tools work. Ann Gulian's warmth and enthusiasm for encouraging learners at all stages shines through in her writing. For students who seek to build a more sophisticated understanding of the mechanisms underlying vocal technique, this book is invaluable."
--- **Dr. Lindsey Leiman**, PSY.D

THE QUINTESSENTIAL
GUIDE TO SINGING

for Voice Teachers and
Very Curious Students

by Ann Gulian

Disclaimer and Copyright

Although the author and publisher have made every effort to ensure that the information presented in this book was correct at press time, the author and publisher do not assume and hereby disclaim any liability to any party for any loss, damage, or disruption caused by errors or omissions, whether such errors or omissions result from negligence, accident, or any other cause.

Copyright © 2022 by Ann Gulian

All rights reserved. This book or any portion thereof may not be reproduced or used in any manner whatsoever without the express written permission of the publisher except for the use of brief quotations in a book review.

Printed in the United States of America

First Printing, 2022

ISBN 979-8-9859315-0-1

For more information, please visit www.anngulianvocalstudio.com

I dedicate this book to my Dad who taught me at a very young age the joy of singing.

Contents

Preface   xii
How to Use This Book   ix

Introduction   1

ENERGY

    Chapter 1   **Posture**   **5**
                         Posture Exercises   8
    Chapter 2   **Breath**   **11**
                         Breath Exercises   13
    Chapter 3   **Breath Support**   **17**
                         Breath Support Exercises   21
    Energy Exercises Summary   **27**
    Energy Review Questions   28
    Troubleshooting   30

VIBRATION

    Chapter 4   **Phonation**   **37**
                         Phonation Exercises   40
    Chapter 5   **Registers**   **43**
                         Register Exercises   46
    Chapter 6   **Register Coordination**   **47**
                         Registration Coordination Exercises   50
    Vibration Exercises Summary   **55**
    Vibration Review Questions   56
    Troubleshooting   57

RESONANCE

    Chapter 7   **Vocal Tract**   **63**
                         Vocal Tract Exercises   70
    Chapter 8   **SOVT Semi-Occluded Vocal Tract**   **79**
                         SOVT Exercises   81
    Chapter 9   **Vowels**   **83**
                         Vowel Exercises   90
    Resonance Exercises Summary   **94**
    Resonance Review Questions   96
    Troubleshooting   99

Sample Warm-ups   103
Bibliography   109
References   113
Index   115
Acknowledgments   119
Exercise tracks   121

Preface

It was not my plan to become a singer. I spent my youth studying classical piano, but when I arrived at the New England Conservatory of Music (NEC) at the age of 17, I finally admitted that hours of practicing Mozart and Bach were not for me. Throughout high school, my outlet had been singing in rock bands and writing songs. Now I was facing a choice; I could be miserable playing classical piano for the next four years, or I could audition for one of the alternative programs offered at NEC. It seemed like a no-brainer! I would become a jazz pianist. There was one problem. I knew very little about jazz piano, but how hard could it be?

My ignorance and arrogance made my weekly "Don't worry! I know what I am doing!!!" phone calls home, ring hollow even to me! As my audition neared, panic set in. So, I did the only thing that made sense to me. I locked myself in practice rooms for hours and sang. This was the therapy that always helped me cope with my feelings and make sense of my thoughts.

After much denial and freaking out, singing for my audition seemed my only logical solution. I sang "Lover Man" and "God Bless the Child" and was accepted into NEC as a jazz vocalist! At that moment, my lifelong obsession with singing began. To be an accomplished singer, I needed to learn the mechanics of singing, which led me to research, study, and dissect the incredible human voice. Teaching forced me to crystallize my knowledge and validated my method.

This book is a culmination of my years of studying and teaching singing. Learning to sing is not a linear process. When learning to sing, we need to be flexible and patient because the mind and body absorb information at different paces. Our intellect may understand a concept before we can physically coordinate it, which is why we practice! One method or approach cannot address every voice's particular concerns and issues because, as individuals, our voices are unique instruments, with unique qualities and needs.

This book focuses on the essential elements of vocal production. You may discover some exercises work like a charm, while others don't. That's fine. Eventually, you will discover the exercises that work best for you. Remember, no one knows your voice better than you!

May 2022

How To Use This Book

VOICE TEACHERS:

Teaching is like the axiom: "Give a man a fish, and you have fed him once. Teach him how to fish and you feed him for a lifetime." As teachers, our goal is to teach each student to understand their voice and to sing with confidence for their entire life.

The foundations of this book will help identify a student's strengths and weaknesses quickly and will simplify the technique of singing. By focusing on each of the three fundamental areas, **ENERGY**, **VIBRATION**, and **RESONANCE**, you will address a student's specific needs.

In my experience, some students are not interested in the "why and how" of singing. They simply want to sing. With those students, I introduce the exercises that I know will help them achieve success, aware that they most likely will not keep all the knowledge. Very often, even these students get to a place of understanding the principles of voice production.

VERY CURIOUS STUDENTS:

Singing is like juggling; we toss and catch each ball slowly until we are juggling fast enough that we can let go and find a comfortable rhythm. Understanding each area of voice production, **ENERGY**, **VIBRATION**, and **RESONANCE**, may feel a bit overwhelming at first. I recommend you preview this book in its entirety before trying the sample warm-ups in the last section of the book. The foundations laid out will help simplify what can seem like a complex physical endeavor. The key to success is to keep in mind the three elements, **ENERGY**, **VIBRATION**, and **RESONANCE**, and to understand how they relate to one another.

Warm up each area of your instrument, beginning with **ENERGY** exercises, then move to **VIBRATION** exercises, and finally, to **RESONANCE** exercises. Be flexible with your warm-up. For example, one day, you may begin your warm-up exercises only to realize that your body is sluggish and could benefit from additional **ENERGY** work before you focus on **VIBRATION** exercises. On another day, when your body feels well aligned, you can move quickly from **ENERGY** and **VIBRATION** exercises to **RESONANCE** exercises. A special note: multiple exercises can combine two areas. For instance, *VOWEL LIFTS* can be a vowel exercise and a breath support exercise. Be clear about what your goal is when practicing each exercise and adjust your practice accordingly.

Listen to yourself objectively but remember, you are learning about your voice, and you should be patient with the results. Too often, we recognize what we dislike about our voice and do not appreciate all the wonderful qualities we already possess. Working with a mirror and recording ourselves are valuable tools and help us assess our progress objectively.

THE QUINTESSENTIAL GUIDE TO SINGING

for Voice Teachers and Very Curious Students

Introduction

Sometimes, singing feels difficult no matter how accomplished the singer is. When we don't understand how our voice works, we may draw incorrect conclusions that lead to temporary solutions. Sometimes, the result can cause frustration and even injury to our voice. There is a logical system for singing. Let's begin by understanding that *every* instrument has three fundamental components.

- an **ENERGY** source

- a **VIBRATORY** source

- a **RESONATING CHAMBER**

For example, when playing the guitar, my fingers are the energy source, the strings are the vibratory source, and the guitar body is the resonating chamber.

The human voice operates similarly. It requires the same three fundamental components: **ENERGY, VIBRATION,** and **RESONANCE.** When singing,

- Our **BREATH** is the energy source

- Our **VOCAL FOLDS** are the vibratory source

- Our **VOCAL TRACT** is the resonating chamber

Understanding how the key elements of singing work and how they relate to one another is imperative to enable our voice to work more efficiently.

Each chapter focuses on one of the fundamental principles, **ENERGY, VIBRATION,** and **RESONANCE,** and includes corresponding exercises. While many of the exercises will be helpful immediately, some may be challenging. That's alright! Be mindful of each exercise's function as you practice.

One last thing before you begin. Our bodies don't respond well to demands. For optimum results, encourage your body to participate rather than command it. I suggest beginning with short, frequent practice sessions, 10 - 20 minutes, multiple times throughout your day, to build stamina and coordination. Practice in a comfortable environment where you can explore your voice freely. Give yourself permission to make mistakes and sound silly; this is how we make discoveries! Be gentle with yourself. Above all, have fun!

ENERGY

POSTURE

1

POSTURE

Your mom was right; don't slouch! Good posture matters! Considering all the physical demands that go into singing a single phrase of music, it is logical that good **BODY ALIGNMENT** improves our ability to sing well. Finding our natural posture before we begin is essential. Without proper body alignment, we impede our ability to take a sufficient breath and to vocalize freely.

A healthy posture should not feel rigid. Keep that in mind as we examine our skeleton and our body's six places of balance: the Atlas-occipital (A-O joint), shoulders, lumbar spine, hips, knees, and ankles.[1]

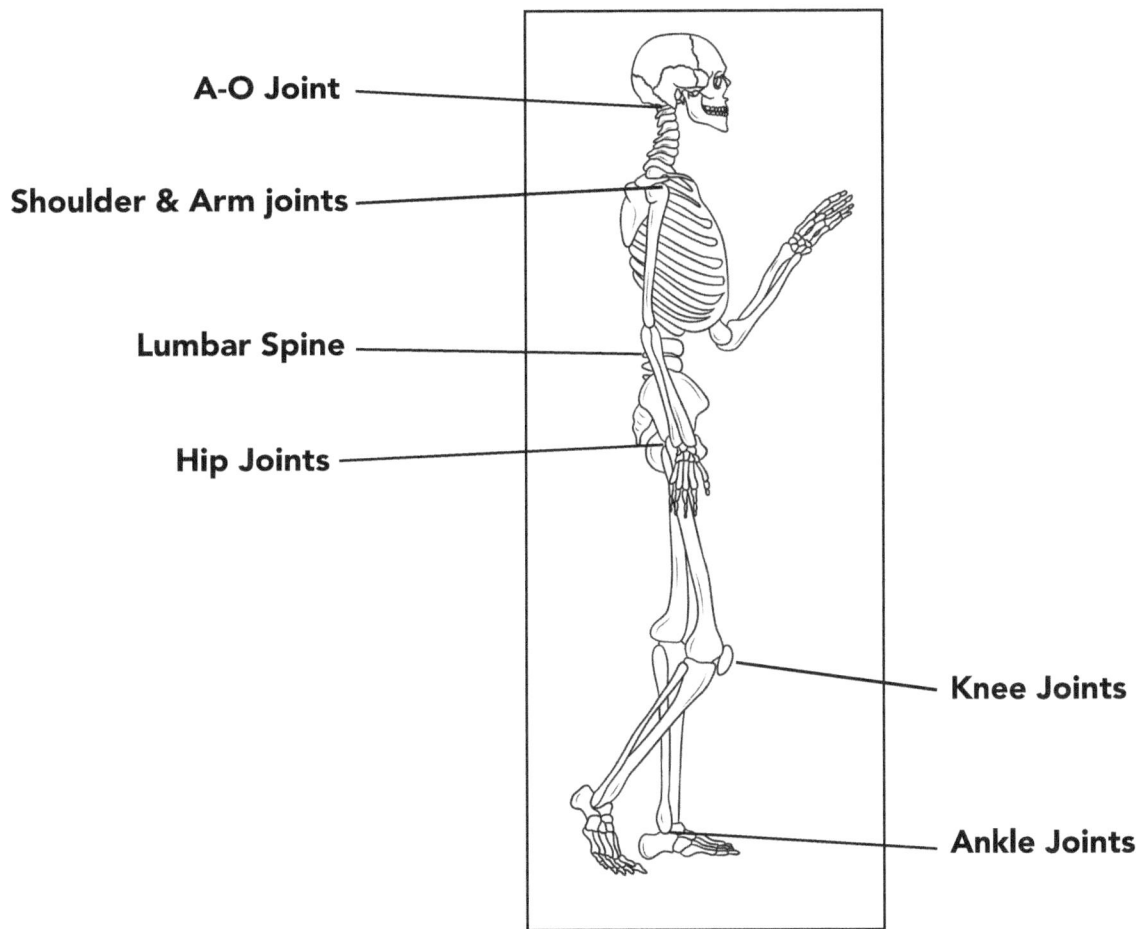

Our spine is one of the primary support structures of our skeleton and the key to good posture.[2] So, what affects our spine and body alignment? Let's begin with our enormous heads!

Our head is like a bowling ball, weighing on average between nine and thirteen pounds.[3] The further an object is from its center of gravity, the more it weighs. Therefore, when our head is "off-balance" and in a forward or backward position, it weighs more and creates unnecessary tension in our shoulders and neck. This tension impacts our ability to become balanced in other areas of our bodies. For this reason, by balancing the base of our skull on the top of our cervical spine at the **ATLAS-OCCIPITAL JOINT (A-O Joint)**, we not only release neck and shoulder tension but achieve better balance.

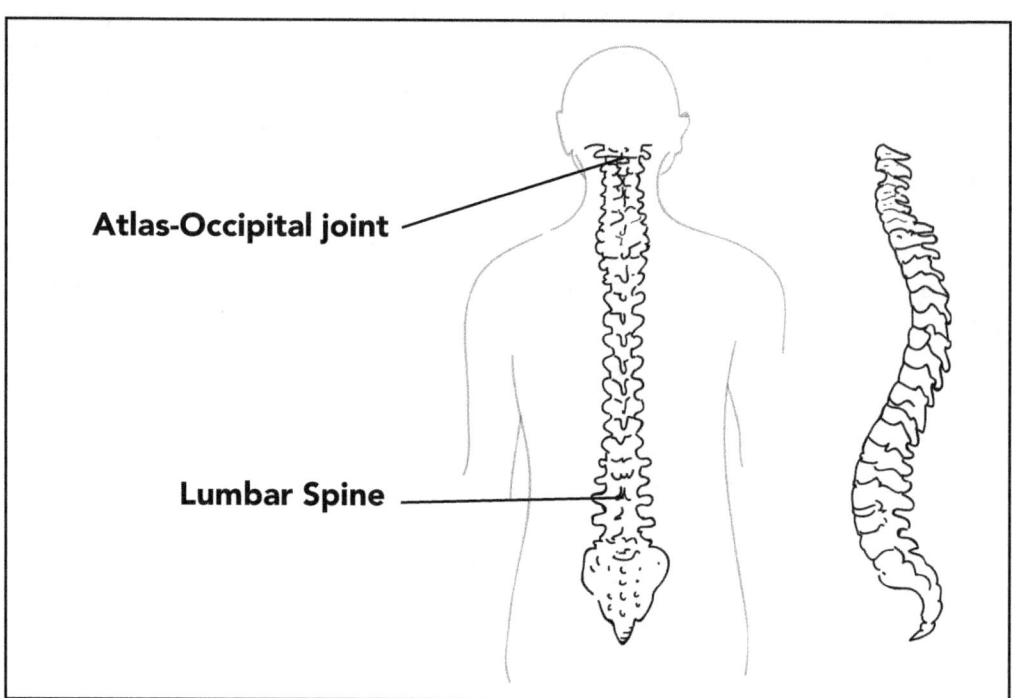

Let's explore balancing our heads at the **ATLAS-OCCIPITAL JOINT**.

* Align your top molars so they are parallel to the floor.[4]
* Imagine your skull is weightless and floating.
* Observe the back of your neck. Does it release?
    - Notice your neck and shoulder muscles relax.
    - Notice your skull is well balanced on the cervical spine.

The **ATLAS-OCCIPITAL JOINT** and the **LUMBAR SPINE** are two primary areas of balance in our spine.[5] Our **LUMBAR SPINE** is the greatest weight-bearing area of our spine, and, like the **ATLAS-OCCIPITAL JOINT**, is in the center of our body.[6] The five lumbar vertebrae support and stabilize our upper body and allow us to move while still maintaining our balance.

To achieve better balance, it is helpful to map the five lumbar vertebrae in our bodies. They are much larger than we think!

Try the following to approximate the circumference of the lumbar vertebrae.

    * Touch your right hand's thumb and pointer to your left hand's thumb and pointer.[7]
        - This approximates the size of your lumbar vertebrae.
    * Try walking forward and backward while picturing your lumbar vertebrae.
        - Your skull should be well-balanced on the cervical spine.

Let's find our body's natural alignment which begins with balancing on our feet.

    * Think of each foot as a tripod with one point of balance near your big toe, one near your pinky toe, and one at your heel.
    * Balancing your weight evenly on each foot, bring your hips over your knees.
    * Next, bring your shoulders over your hips.
    * Finally, bring your ears over your shoulders.
        - Notice any changes in your body's alignment.
        - It's easy to identify issues when we practice with a mirror.

A common image of good body alignment is the carpenter's plumb line. This is a long string with a weight hanging on one end that moves like a pendulum in all directions.

    * Imagine someone holding one end of the plumb line above your head.
    * Think of your body as part of the weighted string.
    * Be sensitive to releasing any spinal compression.

We should practice good body alignment throughout our day. Eventually, our body recalls the sensation of good body alignment, but even with good muscle memory, being mindful of our posture is necessary.

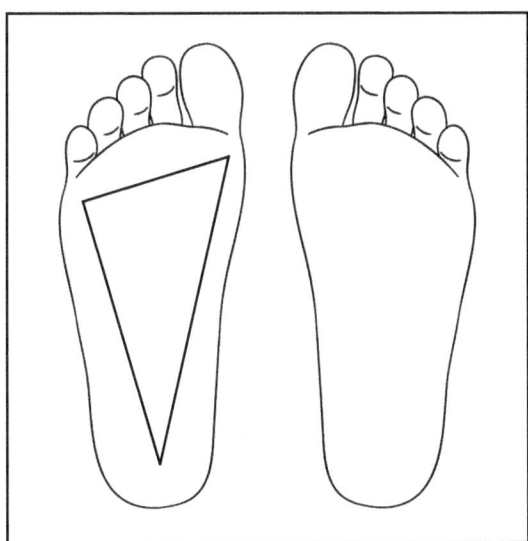
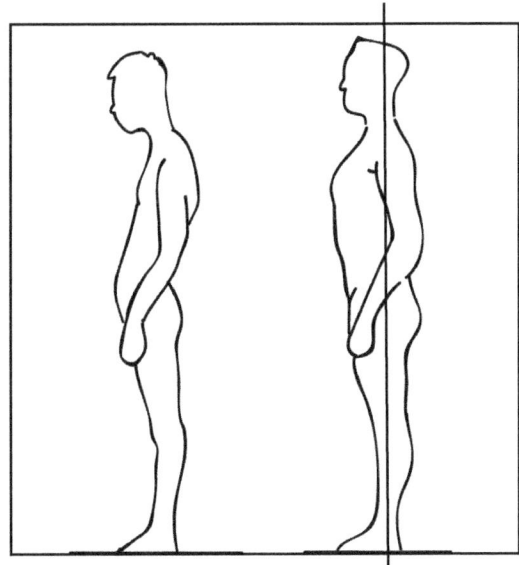

POSTURE EXERCISES

Choose one or two of the following activities for your daily practice.

Activity #1 BODY STRETCH
* Raise both arms as you inhale.
* Take hold of your left wrist; gently pull it towards your right side.
* Feel how your ribs open and expand on your left side as you breathe in and out.
* Repeat this stretch on the other side.

Activity #2 ROLL DOWN
* Roll yourself over until you can touch the floor.
* Hang from your hips and feel how the weight of your head lengthens your neck.
    - Soften your knees if you feel discomfort in your hamstrings.
* Keep your neck relaxed and gently shake your head "no" for a few seconds.
* Next, nod your head "yes" as if it is a pendulum for a few seconds.
* When you are ready, gradually roll up, stacking one vertebrae on top of another.

Activity #3 LINE IT UP
* Balance your weight evenly on each foot.
* Bring your ears over your shoulders to align them.
* Bring your shoulders over your hips.
* Bring your hips over your knees.
* Bring your knees over your ankles.

Activity #4 DESCRIPTIVE WORDS[8]
Every time we stand, gravity compresses our vertebrae. Descriptive words, like "floating" or "expansive", can help us recall the sensation of releasing any spinal compression, as well as mapping our A-O joint and lumbar spine.

* Make a list of descriptive words that help remind you to release your spine.

Activity #5 THE SAUCER
* Visualize your pelvic girdle as a teacup and saucer.
* Adjust your balance so your pelvic girdle does not tip and "spill the tea".
* Walk around your space while keeping your pelvic girdle level.
* Be aware of your lumbar spine supporting you as you move.

Activity #6 HEAD TURNS
* Maintaining a well-balanced head, slowly turn your head to the right as you sing.
    - Note if your posture shifts out of alignment and re-adjust as necessary.
* Maintaining a well-balanced head, slowly turn your head to the left as you sing.
    - Note if your posture shifts out of alignment and re-adjust as necessary.
* Repeat several times.

Activity #7 *NECK ROLLS*
* Keep your shoulders level as you drop your chin to your chest.
* Roll your head to the right bringing your right ear towards your right shoulder.
* Feel the stretch on the left side of your neck and shoulder.
* Drop your your chin towards your chest again.
* Roll your head to the left bringing your left ear towards your left shoulder.
* Feel the stretch on the right side of your neck and shoulder.
* Repeat this semi-circle movement several times.

Activity #8 *YWTL*
These stretches are formulated by a chiropractor, and I like how they open the chest and align our spine.

* Stand with both arms raised, making a "Y" shape with your palms facing forward.
* Gently pull your arms back and hold for 15 - 30 seconds.
* Next, make a "W" shape with your arms by bringing your elbows down slightly.
* Keep your hands at shoulder height and hold for 15 - 30 seconds.
* Now, make a "T" shape by bringing your arms out to the side.
* Palms should still be facing forward as you hold for 15 - 30 seconds.
* Finally, make an "L" shape by bringing your elbows down to your waist.
* Hold for 30 seconds.

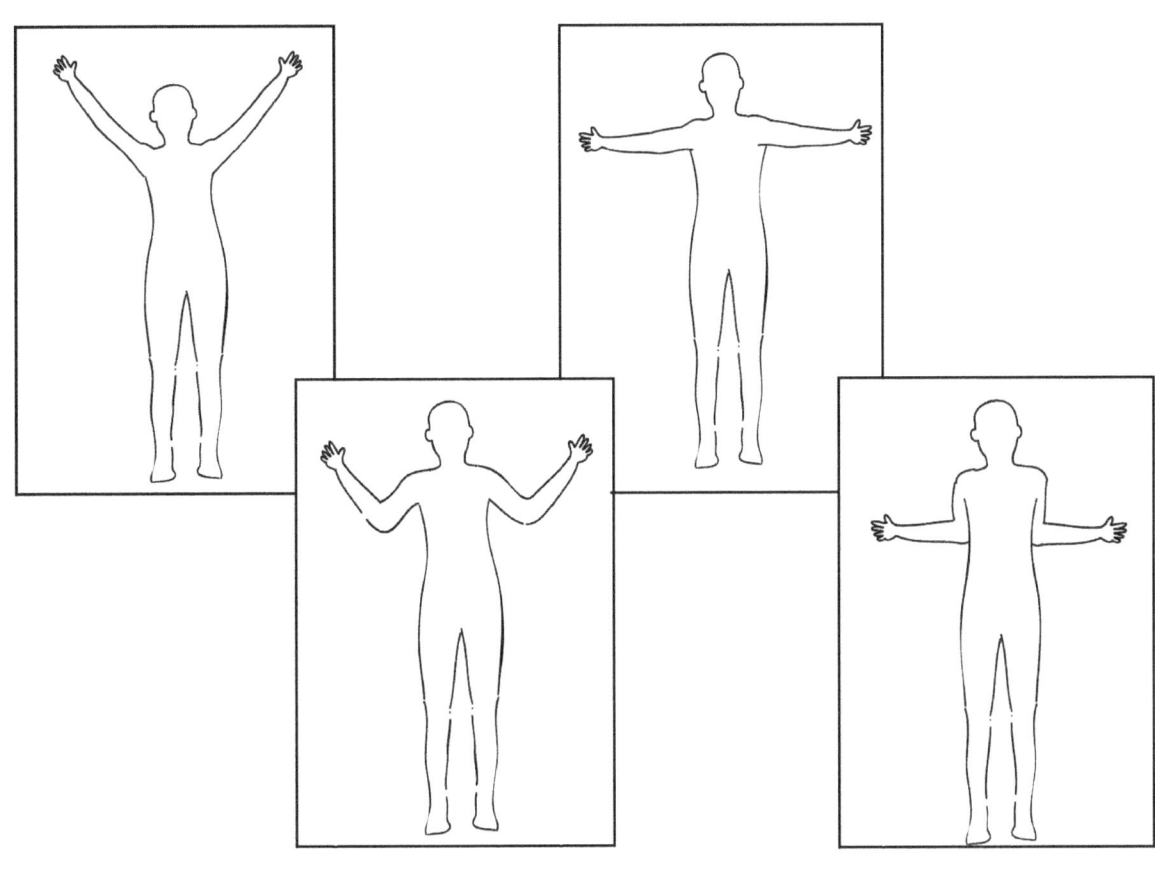

2

BREATH

Our breath sustains life, and like our heartbeat, often our breath happens without a conscious thought. It is the engine of our voice. Every inhale must be sufficient, and every exhale must coordinate to produce the sound we wish for the time we desire. We must learn to inhale quickly, then exhale slowly and steadily as we sing.

Our lungs fill and *hold* our breath, but the muscles surrounding our lungs *control* our breath. The **DIAPHRAGM MUSCLE** is a muscular sheet shaped like an upside-down bowl. It operates like a bellows pump, drawing air into the lungs and expelling air out of the lungs. Think of the diaphragm as a pancake or trampoline separating the abdominal and chest cavities. This muscular sheet attaches to the sternum in the front, to the intercostal muscles along the lower rib cage, to the lumbar vertebrae in the back, and to the lungs at their base. If you place your fingers underneath the edge of your front ribs, you can feel your diaphragm's movement as you breathe.

The diaphragm's full range of motion moves air in and out of our lungs. The diaphragm and lungs work like an accordion. When we inhale, the diaphragm descends, acting like an expanding accordion. As it pulls our lungs open, air rushes in to fill them. Conversely, when the diaphragm rises, it puts pressure under our lungs and empties them, similar to someone compressing the bellows of an accordion.

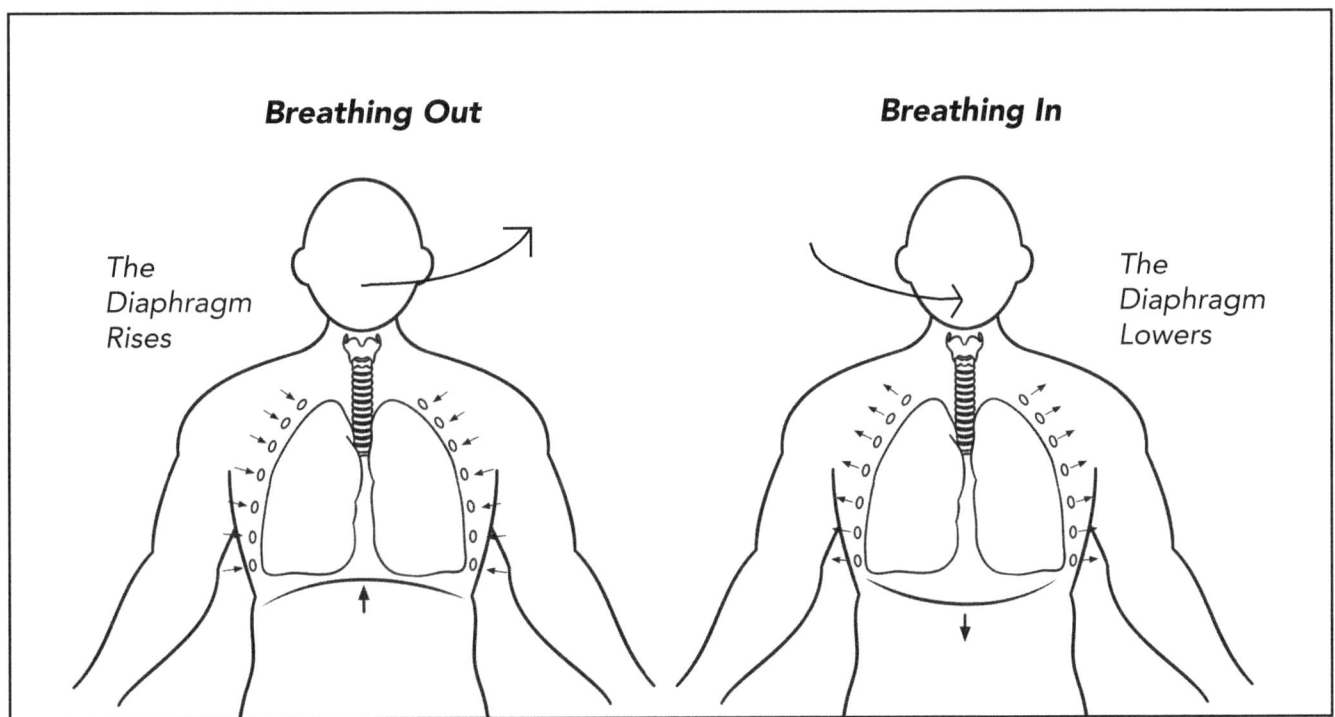

However, the diaphragm is an unpaired muscle. This means it depends on other muscles to help it move, specifically, the **INTERCOSTAL MUSCLES**, which are the set of muscles between our ribs. When the **EXTERNAL INTERCOSTAL MUSCLES** contract, they pull our ribs up and widen them, helping the diaphragm's downward movement and our lungs expand. When the **INTERNAL INTERCOSTALS** contract, our ribcage narrows, and the diaphragm returns to its dome shape, emptying the air from our lungs.

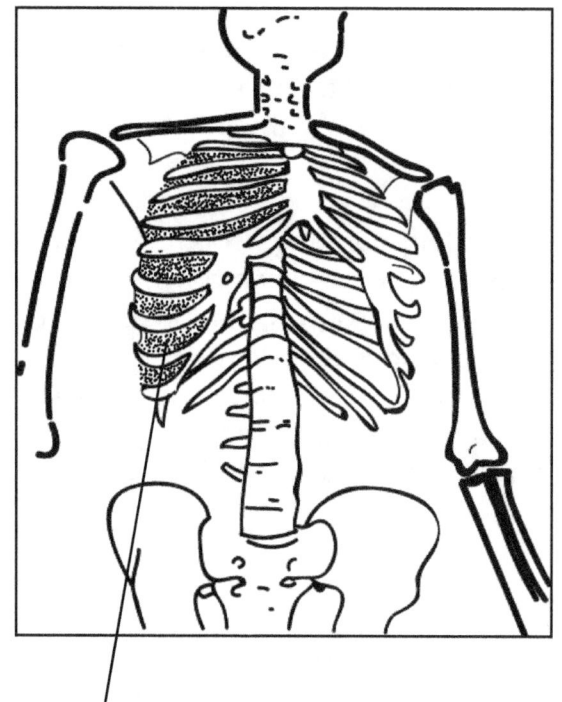

Intercostal muscles from the front

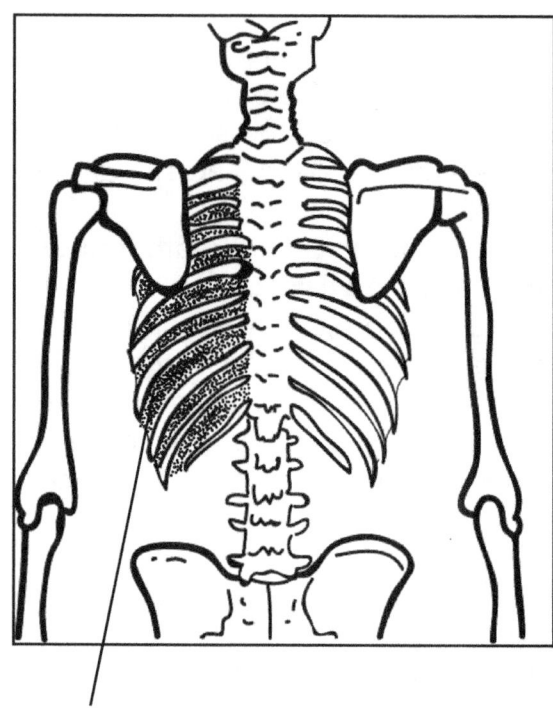

Intercostal muscles from the back

* Place your hands on the sides of your ribcage and inhale.
* Visualize your intercostal muscles expanding your ribs.
* Now, exhale and visualize your intercostal muscles narrowing your ribs.
    - Keep in mind that your ribs attach to your spine, and as the ribs move, so must your spine.
* Notice your thoracic spine "gathering" as your ribs lift on the inhale and "lengthening" as your ribs lower on the exhale.[9]
* Pay special attention to keeping your shoulders and arms relaxed as you breathe.

You often hear the phrase "breathe into your belly". As we know, this is physically impossible! So why is this such a common direction for singers? It is because our diaphragm contracts downward, flattening as we inhale, and it displaces our internal organs. Our abdomen must expand to make room for the displaced viscera. We inhibit our diaphragm's ability to descend if we do not relax our belly on the inhalation. Fortunately, we are quite familiar with the feeling of "breathing into our belly" because we do this when we sleep.

Now that we have a better understanding of how our diaphragm, intercostals, and abdominal muscles function when we breathe, let's practice!

BREATH EXERCISES

Choose one or two of the following activities for your daily practice.

Activity #9 DIAPHRAGM AWARENESS
* Laying on the floor, bring your knees towards the ceiling.
* Place your hands on your abdomen and breathe normally.
* Observe your hands rise and lower with every breath you take.
* Visualize your diaphragm contracting downward as you inhale and releasing upward as you exhale.

Inhale   *Exhale*

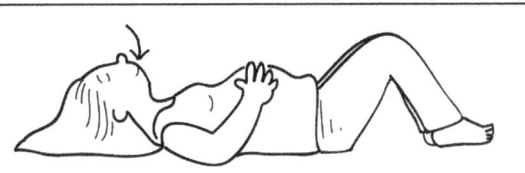 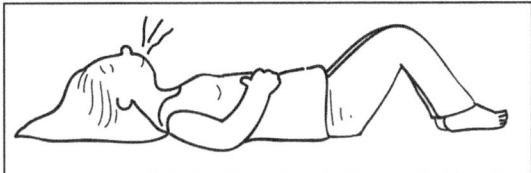

Activity #10 SMELL THE BREAD
* Imagine you are smelling the aroma of the most delicious bread baking in the oven.
* Keep your shoulders down and inhale no higher than your armpits.
* Visualize your diaphragm descending as you inhale.

Activity #11 BACK BREATHING
* Seated in a chair, lean your torso forward at the waist.
* Drop your head between your legs.
* With your hands on your lower back, breathe in and feel your waist expand.
* Exhale and feel your waist narrow.
* Stand with your hands on your lower back.
* Focus on breathing into your lower back.
* Exhale making an /S/ sound (aka exhaling on an /S/) while maintaining some expansion with your lower back ribs.

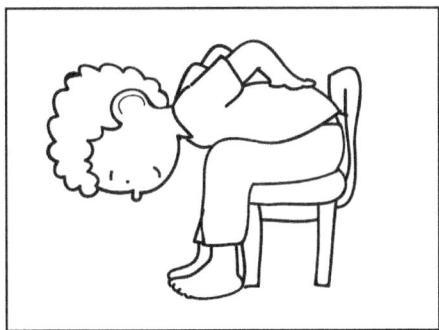

Activity #12 SUSPEND THE BREATH[10]
Our singing breath has four phases; inhalation, suspension, exhalation, and recovery. The suspension phase conflicts with our body's natural habit to control air pressure by closing the glottis (the space between our vocal folds).

* Inhale for 4 counts.
* Maintain an open throat or glottis as you suspend your breath for 4 more counts.
* Now exhale normally.
* Pause, then begin the next cycle.
* Inhale for 3 counts, suspend for 3 counts, and exhale normally.
* Pause, then begin the next cycle.
* Inhale for 2 counts, suspend for 2 counts, and exhale your breath.
* Pause, then begin your last cycle.
* Inhale for 1 count, suspend for 1 count, and exhale.

Activity #13 VACUUM THE LUNGS[11]
* Exhale your breath completely.
* Plug your nose and close your mouth.
* With your nose plugged and mouth closed, go through the motions of inhaling.
* Continue going through the motions of inhaling as you move and bend your body in all directions.
* Let go of your nose and open your mouth and throat when you feel you must inhale and can no longer resist.
* Allow the air to rush into your lungs and fill the vacuum.

Activity #14 NOSE BREATHING[12]
Each of the following activities requires you to take in enough air without over inhaling.

A
* Inhale through your nose for 4 count.
* Exhale through your nose for 4 counts.
* Repeat several times.

B
* Inhale through your nose for 4 counts.
* Exhale through your nose for 8 counts.
* Repeat several times.

C
* Exhale through the nose quickly as if you are coughing or laughing.
* Relax your belly and let the breath enter your body without conscious effort.
* This is one breath cycle. Repeat the cycle twenty times.

Activity #15 PULL THE STRING
* *Slowly* pull an imaginary string from your mouth while exhaling on an /S/.
    - You should be out of breath by the time your arm is completely extended.
* Repeat.

Activity #16 THE ALPHABET EXERCISE
Imagine you have hiccups and want to get rid of them by "holding" your breath. There is only one catch! You must keep your throat open while "holding" your breath. This requires you to engage your intercostal muscles in order to suspend your breath while your vocal folds and larynx remain relaxed. Try the following exercise with this in mind.

* Speak the alphabet as many times as possible while suspending your breath.
* Keep the breath pressure low in your body and away from your vocal folds.

Activity #17 GOAL POST
We are helping our intercostals engage by lifting our arms.

* Using a chair, sit on your "sitting bones".
* Create a goal post with your arms by raising them or placing your hands on your head.
* Inhale feeling your waist expand.
* Exhale on an /S/.
* Sing a song with your hands raised.

Activity #18 "8-8-16"[13]
* Exhale completely.
* Next, inhale slowly through your nose keeping your shoulders down for 8 counts.
* Suspend your breath for 8 counts.
    - Remember to engage your intercostals!
* Exhale slowly through your mouth for 16 counts, until completely empty.
* Repeat.

If "8-8-16" is too challenging, begin with "4-4-8" and work your way up. Gradually increase your count to "10-10-20". *For an extra challenge, do this exercise while walking.*

Activity #19 ELEVATOR DOWN
* Inhale.
* Visualize your diaphragm as an elevator lowering to the basement (your pelvic floor).
* Exhale on an /S/ and imagine the elevator slowly rising.
* Repeat, but this time sing an /OO/ as you visualize the elevator slowly rising.

Activity #20 FILL THE VACUUM
Tune into the small skeletal movements your body makes with each breath cycle.

* Inhale by opening your throat and relaxing your belly as the air "comes to you" and fills your lungs.
* Exhale observing the gentle pressure your abs and ribs make.
* Repeat the cycle.
    - Do not "pull" or "draw your breath" as you inhale.

Activity #21 SQUAT BREATHS
* Squat down and place your hands on the floor in front of you.
* Take a breath and "breathe into your buttocks".
* Observe any sensations in your sacrum and pelvic floor.
* Stand and "breathe into your buttocks".
* Observe any sensations in your sacrum and pelvic floor.

Activity #22 INTERCOSTAL STRETCHES[14]

A

* Inhale raising both your arms.
* Press your hands together in a prayer position.
* Exhale on an /S/.
* Flex your intercostal muscles.
* Repeat this stretch a few times.

B
* Lace your fingers and turn your palms outward.
* Inhale.
* Press your palms forward.
* Engage your intercostal muscles as you exhale on an /S/.
* Repeat this stretch a few times.

C

* Lace your fingers behind your back.
* Pull your hands away from your buttocks.
* Feel the stretch in your chest.
* Inhale.
* Keep your chest expanded as you exhale on an /S/.
* Repeat this stretch a few times.

3

BREATH SUPPORT

Breath support is the dynamic relationship between our breath and our vocal folds (vocal cords). We must take a sufficient inhale and manage or regulate our exhale to produce the sound we wish for the time we desire. To manage our breath is to control our breath, and control often leads to tension. For this reason, it is helpful to think of breath support as to how our breath "influences" our **VOCAL FOLDS**, or vocal cords.[15]

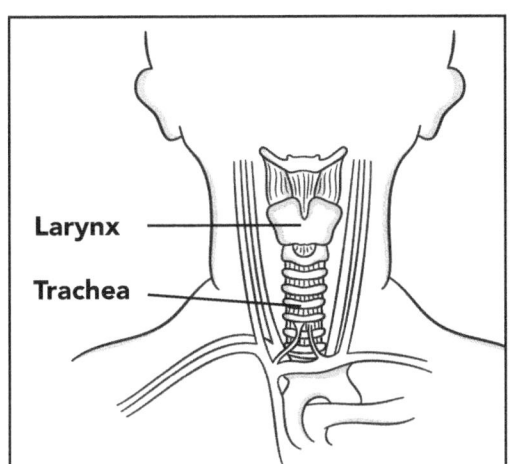
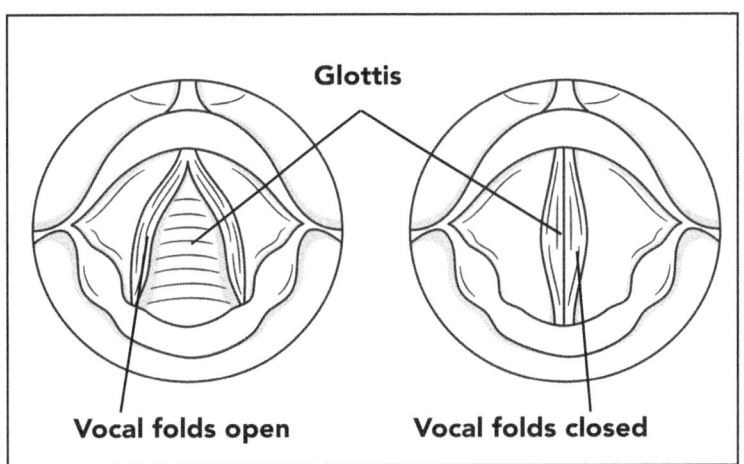

If you place your finger on the front of your throat and swallow, you will feel a bump. This is your **LARYNX**, which is commonly called the voice box or the "Adam's Apple". It is roughly the size of a walnut.[16]

Inside our larynx are two muscles called the vocal folds. They stretch across the larynx horizontally from front to back. The space between our vocal folds is called the **GLOTTIS**, which opens and closes to allow air in and out of our lungs. When we sing, the glottis closes and our outgoing breath meets resistance at our vocal folds. This resistance vibrates them and produces sound.

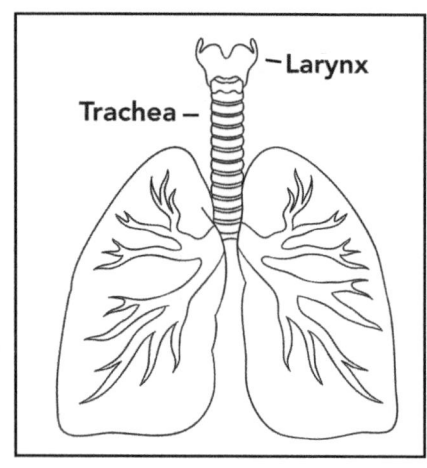

Imagine that the air in both of our lungs is like 4 lanes of highway merging into a single lane, which is our **TRACHEA** or windpipe. The vocal folds, located in our larynx at the top of the trachea, would be under a lot of pressure as the 4 lanes merge. If our breath support muscles don't help "direct traffic" and slow down the amount of breath entering our windpipe, there will be a "traffic jam". This traffic jam, or extreme **SUBGLOTTIC PRESSURE** under the vocal folds, creates tension in our vocal folds as they connect, like when we yell.

CLAVICULAR BREATHING is a common cause of this "traffic jam". When singers inhale by lifting their shoulders and collarbones, their diaphragm does not descend completely, making exhalation difficult to regulate. The result is extreme subglottic pressure under the vocal folds.

To help reverse this problematic breathing, we must encourage our diaphragm to descend fully on the inhalation. We do this is by opening our glottis and relaxing our abdominal muscles, which then allows the diaphragm to lower, filling our lungs with air. This is contrary to many people's habit of "drawing a breath". Instead, we must practice allowing the air to come to us.

Our ability to regulate our breath and allow our vocal folds to vibrate without tension requires us to play with our breath's flow *(air stream)* and resistance to the flow *(breath pressure)*.[17] We must coordinate the amount of air we take in with the musical phrase being sung. If we don't take in enough air, we may run out of breath. If we take in too much air, we feel as if we are holding our breath and must empty our lungs before the next inhale. To create enough breath pressure but not overwhelm our vocal folds requires practice.

Let's begin by examining the differences between the pressure of a small inhalation and the pressure of a large inhalation.[18]

* Hold a shallow breath for 10 seconds.
    - You may feel desperate for air, but notice your breathing muscles are not working hard to suspend the breath.

* Now, hold a deep breath for 10 seconds.
    - You may feel you have plenty of air, but notice your breathing muscles are working harder to suspend the breath.
    - Notice there is pressure under your vocal folds.

In Chapter 2, we learned how the diaphragm muscle functions like an accordion, helping to pull air into our lungs. We also learned that our **ABDOMINAL MUSCLES** must relax as we inhale to allow our diaphragm's full downward contraction. Since our diaphragm is an unpaired muscle, it depends on other muscles, like the intercostal muscles, to help it descend on the inhale and relax on the exhale.

Our diaphragm muscle, intercostal muscles, abdominal muscles, and pelvic floor muscles make up an **"INNER ABDOMINAL CANISTER"**. Along with the spine, pelvis, and lower rib cage, they form a "container of air pressure" in our torso. We learn how to manipulate this "container of air" to regulate our airflow.

Let's look closer at the muscles that make up this "container". The **RECTUS ABDOMINIS**, or "six-pack" muscle, lies just beneath the surface of our skin. Layered underneath are the **EXTERNAL OBLIQUES** and the **INTERNAL OBLIQUES**. Underneath these muscles is the **TRANSVERSE ABDOMINAL**. *This deep lying muscle wraps around our body horizontally like a corset and stabilizes our torso.*

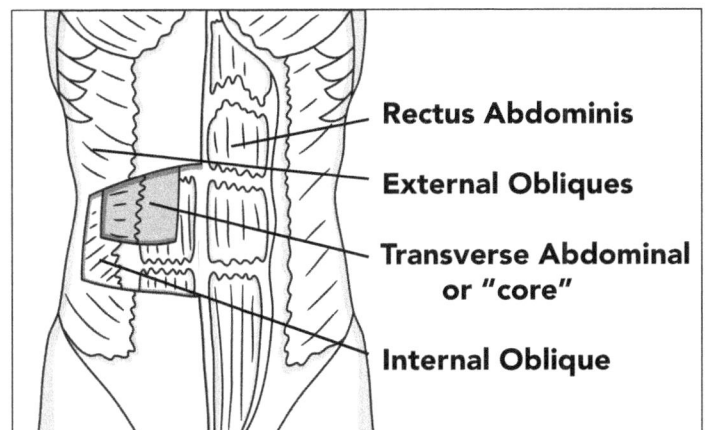
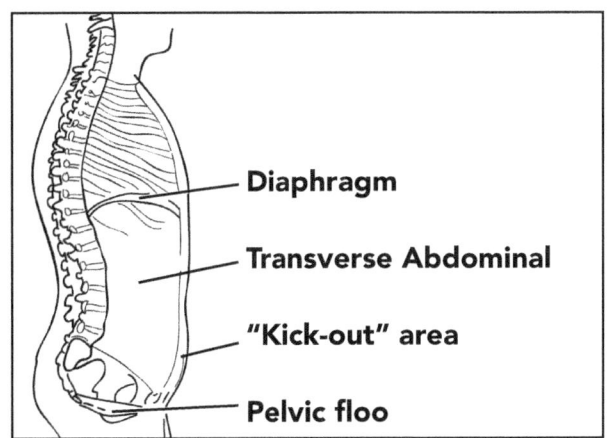

We often refer to our transverse abdominal muscle as our **CORE**. It is like an internal weight belt. In fact, when weightlifters need power, they engage this muscle while closing their glottis. We innately engage our core and close our glottis regularly in our daily lives. Every time we lift a heavy object, we close our glottis as we bear down. We also do this while performing daily bodily functions. A woman closes her glottis when bearing down to give birth. The result of closing the glottis is more breath pressure and more power.

How we engage our **"INNER ABDOMINAL CANISTER"** muscles takes some experimentation. Some vocal pedagogies refer to the **"KICK-OUT" AREA**[19], which is the portion of our abdomen just below where a belt would lie. When we engage our "kick out" area, we are actually engaging our core.

To find the "kick-out" area:

> * Place your hand on your abdomen, just below where your belt would lie, and make a small cough.
>> - No doubt you felt your abs engage. If not, move your hand lower on your abdomen until you feel movement.
>
> * Once you have located this, giggle silently as if you are trying not to laugh.
>
> * Notice your lower belly "kick out".
>> - It takes a little time to coordinate the "kick out" action, so be patient.

Spend some time getting used to the sensation of the "kick out", and observe how the other abdominal muscles react. Remember, our goal is to coordinate varying degrees of "resistance" with our inner abdominal canister.

Our **PELVIC FLOOR** has an equally important role in stabilizing our diaphragm since it is the bottom of the inner abdominal canister. The pelvic floor is a group of muscles that stretch like a hammock from our pubic bone to our tailbone and from one sitting bone to the other. These muscles create a shallow bowl shape that mirrors the diaphragm. When the diaphragm descends, so does the pelvic floor as it responds to the increased pressure by lengthening.

As a quick experiment, try lifting a heavy object like a piano or table and observe any sensations in your pelvic floor. No doubt you felt some pressure. Now locate and engage your "kick-out" area with a stifled cough or giggle. Observe any sensations of pressure on your pelvic floor. This is because all of the muscles of the "inner abdominal canister" work in tandem.

The last area of importance is the **EPIGASTRIUM**, which is not a muscle but is the portion of the upper abdomen right below the sternum where the diaphragm and sternum connect. Picture your entire torso as a balloon. When we squeeze the bottom of a balloon, the displaced air inside causes the balloon to bulge at the top. Our epigastrium responds to the increased breath pressure of the inner abdominal canister by bulging at the top as the balloon does. Effective vocal warm-ups can begin with /SH/ to activate the epigastric area. We call it "jumping" or "bouncing" the epigastrium. It is a simple and effective way to wake up our core. Important to note, when we "jump" the epigastrium, we do not "pull in" our lower abdomen; we engage our "kick-out" area and pelvic floor.

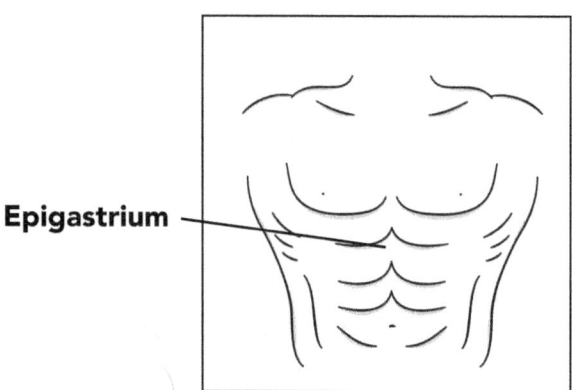

Keeping our breath pressure low in our body allows the vocal folds to meet without overwhelming them. For this reason, "sitting on the breath" is a common image used to keep the breath pressure low in our body.

By continually playing with our breath's *flow* and *resistance to the flow*[20] we learn to create enough subglottic pressure to vibrate our vocal folds yet not overwhelm them when we sing. Work with these concepts as you explore how your breath's energy influences your voice, always remembering to regulate your outgoing breath and allow your vocal folds to vibrate freely.

BREATH SUPPORT EXERCISES

Choose one or two of the following exercises for your daily practice.

Activity #23 **LESS IS MORE**
* Take a shallow inhale and hold 5 seconds.
* Observe how your breathing muscles remain relaxed.
* Exhale.
* Now take a deep inhale and hold for 5 seconds.
* Observe how your breathing muscles are more active.
* Exhale.
* Next, open your glottis and relax your abdomen, allowing the air to come to you.
   - Be mindful that you do not over inhale.
* Without using more energy than is necessary, exhale on /SH/.
* Repeat, playing with the amount of air you take in.

Activity #24 **HUSH!**
* Place your hand on your epigastrium and hold /SH/ for 4 counts.
* Then, hold /F/ for 4 counts.
* Continue alternating /SH/ and /F/ for 4 counts each.

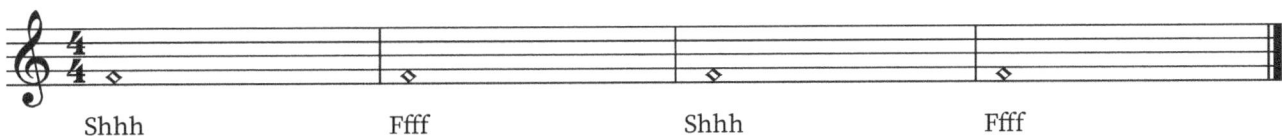

Activity #25 **QUIET, PLEASE!**
* Place your hand on your epigastrium and alternate /SH/ and /S/ with the pattern below.
* Bounce your epigastrium.
* Keep a light staccato as you sing.

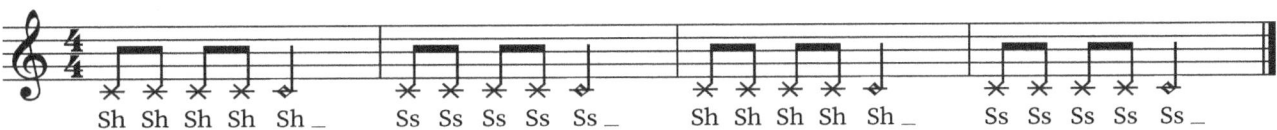

Activity #26 **INFLATE A BALLOON**
I suggest using your imagination with this activity rather than inflating a real balloon which can create neck tension.

* Feel your core activate as you pretend to inflate a balloon.

Activity #27 LIFT THE PIANO
* Try lifting a piano or desk as you sing.
* Observe how your core muscles engage and your vocal folds connect easily.
* Sit in a chair.
* Remain seated and try lifting the chair seat with your hands.
* Observe how your core muscles engage and your vocal folds connect easily.

Activity #28 LAT PULL-DOWN
Pretend you are at the gym and pulling down a horizontal bar.

* Create resistance as you pull-down.
    - You should feel your core muscles engage.
* Try singing as you engage your core.

Activity #29 PLANKS & BELTS
There are many activities, such as pilates, that engage our core.

* Hold your body in a plank position.
* Feel your transverse abdominal muscle activate.
* Stand and wrap a wide exercise band or a belt around your waist.
* Keep your core engaged and pressing against the band or belt as you exhale on an /S/.

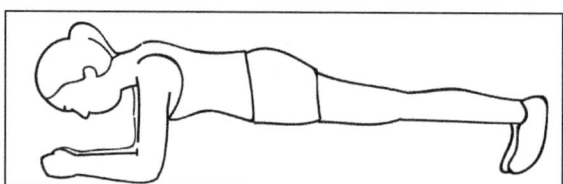

Activity #30 HUG THE BEACH BALL
This exercise helps identify and engage our intercostal muscles.

* Imagine you are hugging a beach ball.
* Gently press the heels of your hands together while exhaling on /S/.
* Observe how your intercostal muscles "flex" as you press your hands.

Activity #31 INHALE WHILE YOU SING
* Sing on "the gesture" of inhalation as you sing.
* Continue to imagine you are inhaling while singing.

Activity #32 KNEE BENDS
This action engages our "inner abdominal canister" muscles.

* Make a small squat or knee bend as you sing.
* Observe any increased ease with closing your glottis.

Activity #33 ROLLS
Moving your body can help release your breath.

* Roll your shoulders as you sing.
* Make circles with your hips as you sing.

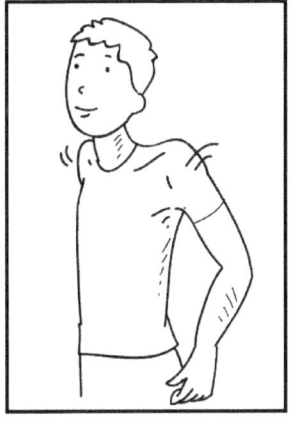

Activity #34 DRAWING CIRCLES
This activity engages our core while freeing our breath.

* Extend both of your arms out to the front.
* Imagine your pointer fingers are pencils.
* Moving your arms from your shoulders, draw circles with your fingers and sing.
* Observe the engagement of your core muscles.

Activity #35 BOOK ON BELLY[21]
* Lie on your back with your knees up and your feet flat on the floor.
* Place a book on the "kick-out" area of your abdomen.
* Inhale and observe that the book rises.
* Activate your "kick-out" muscle to keep the book elevated while **counting out loud** to 15.
* Next, sing a note and **count out loud** to 15.
* Overtime, gradually increase your count to 30.

Activity #36 TEETH BREATHING
* Make an /S/ sound as you inhale through your teeth.
* Identify your core and how it engages.
* Keep your core active as you exhale on an /S/.
* Repeat

Activity #37 SHAKE HANDS
* Clasp your hands in front.
* Shake your hands quickly to free your breath while singing.

Activity #38 EPIGASTRIUM MASSAGE
* Make a fist with your right hand.
* Place your fist on your epigastrium.
* Place your left hand over your fist.
* Massage your fist gently into your epigastrium as you sing.
    - This action will free your breath while singing.

Activity #39 CRESCENDO
* Sing an /OO/ quietly.
* Crescendo, gradually getting louder by engaging your core support muscles.
    - Be careful to not engage your larynx to get louder!
* Decrescendo, gradually getting softer.

Activity #40 ABDOMINAL PULSES
* Lie with your knees towards the ceiling and your feet flat on the floor.
* Place a book on your "kick-out" area and pulse the book towards the ceiling on the accents.
* Alternate with a /SH/ and a /HUM/.

Activity #41 KICK-OUT LIFTS [22]
* Lie with your knees towards the ceiling and your feet flat on the floor.
* Place a book on your "kick-out" area.
* Observe your entire "inner abdominal canister" as you gently press the book towards the ceiling on the ascending 5th.

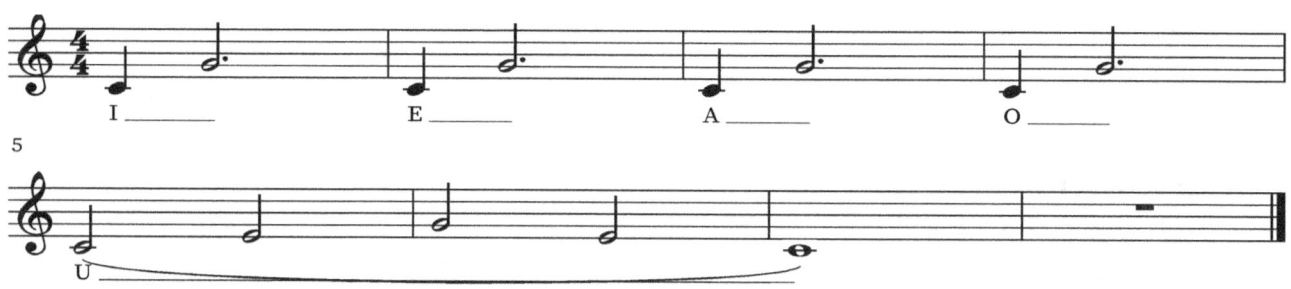

Activity #42 LA ROSA
* Imagine throwing a frisbee across a football field as you sing.

Activity #43 ARM LIFTS
* Exhale completely.
* Then inhale, raising both your arms overhead.
* sing and imagine "wasting your breath" as you sustain the irst note.
* Lower your arms as you continue singing the descending arpeggio.

Exhale   Inhale   Oo

EXERCISES

Record your own exercises here.

ENERGY EXERCISES SUMMARY

POSTURE
1. BODY STRETCH — p.8
2. ROLL DOWN — p.8
3. LINE IT UP — p.8
4. DESCRIPTIVE WORDS — p.8
5. THE SAUCER — p.8
6. HEAD TURNS — p.8
7. NECK ROLLS — p.9
8. YWTL — p.9

BREATH
9. DIAPHRAGM AWARENESS — p.13
10. SMELL THE BREAD — p.13
11. BACK BREATHING — p.13
12. SUSPEND THE BREATH — p.14
13. VACUUM THE LUNGS — p.14
14. NOSE BREATHING — p.14
15. PULL THE STRING — p.14
16. THE ALPHABET EXERCISE — p.15
17. GOAL POST — p.15
18. "8-8-16" — p.15
19. ELEVATOR DOWN — p.15
20. FILL THE VACUUM — p.15
21. SQUAT BREATHS — p.16
22. INTERCOSTAL STRETCHES — p.16

BREATH SUPPORT
23. LESS IS MORE — p.21
24. HUSH! — p.21
25. QUIET, PLEASE! — p.21
26. INFLATE A BALLOON — p.21
27. LIFT THE PIANO — p.22
28. LAT PULL-DOWN — p.22
29. PLANKS AND BELTS — p.22
30. HUG THE BEACH BALL — p.22
31. INHALE WHILE YOU SING — p.22
32. KNEE BENDS — p.22
33. ROLLS — p.23
34. DRAWING CIRCLES — p.23
35. BOOK ON BELLY — p.23
36. TEETH BREATHING — p.23
37. SHAKE HANDS — p.23
38. EPIGASTRIUM MASSAGE — p.23
39. CRESCENDO — p.24
40. ABDOMINAL PULSES — p.24
41. KICK-OUT LIFTS — p.24
42. LA ROSA — p.24
43. ARM LIFTS — p.25

ENERGY REVIEW QUESTIONS

1. What are the three foundational principles of voice production?
 * Energy (breath or air), Vibration (vocal folds) and Resonance (vocal tract).

2. What is the goal of a well-aligned posture?
 * To balance our weight and lengthen our spine so that no muscle or muscle groups work harder than necessary which allows our breath to be efficient.

3. What are the two main points of balance in the spine?
 * The atlas-occipital joint and the lumbar spine.

4. What are the four primary breathing muscles?
 * The diaphragm muscle, the intercostal muscles, the abdominal muscles, and the pelvic floor muscles.

5. Describe the diaphragm and its action for both inhalation and exhalation.
 * The diaphragm is a dome-shaped muscle housed in the thoracic cavity that contracts downward on the inhalation and relaxes back to its dome shape upon exhalation.

6. Describe the intercostal muscles and how they function.
 * Located between the ribs, their contraction and expansion allow the ribcage to move freely.

7. How do the abdominal muscles function during respiration?
 * They release on the inhalation and engage on the exhalation.

8. How do the pelvic floor muscles function during respiration?
 * They mirror the diaphragm.

9. What happens to the vocal folds if we use too much breath when singing?
 * Too forceful a breath can create tension in the vocal folds and surrounding area as they try to connect and vibrate.

10. Where is the "kick out" muscle located?
 * In the mid to lower belly area below the naval.

11. What are two ways to identify the "kick-out" muscle area?
 * Pretend you are going to cough or suppress a giggle.

13. What is subglottic pressure?
   When the breath from our lungs meets our vocal folds and vibrates them.

14. What is breath management?
   How fast or slow we release our breath.

15. What muscles make up the "inner abdominal canister"?
   The diaphragm muscle, the transverse abdominis muscle, the intercostal muscles, and the pelvic floor muscles.

TROUBLESHOOTING

CHAPTER 1 - POSTURE

1. Is your head tilted? Is your chin too high or low? [23]
   Place your right thumb on the bottom of your top front teeth.
   Place your left index finger at the base of your skull.
   Rock your head up and down. You should notice that your neck releases, and your skull moves more easily.
   - *Note that your head comes to rest parallel with the floor and feels balanced and buoyant.*
   Next, place your right thumb on the edge of your chin.
   Place your left index finger at the base of your skull.
   Rock your skull up and down with your hands.
   - *Remember to let your hands do all the work!*

2. Are your shoulders raised or uneven? Are you slumping with a collapsed chest?
   Work in front of the mirror to check your body's alignment.

3. Is there too much curvature at the base of your back? Is your balance off? Are your knees locked?
   Use the "Line It Up" exercise to explore what feels comfortable for you.

CHAPTER 2 - BREATHING

1. Are you taking a clavicular inhale and lifting your shoulders as you inhale?
   Keep your shoulders down as you inhale.
   - *This allows your diaphragm to descend fully on the inhale.*

2. Are you pulling the air into your lungs rather than letting the air come to you?
   Practice opening your glottis on the inhalation and relaxing your abdomen to fill your lungs.

3. Is your posture collapsing as you exhale or sing?
   Practice the "Goal Post" exercise and keep your breast bone level.

CHAPTER 3 - BREATH SUPPORT

1. Are you tensing your lower abdomen as you sing?
The goal is to regulate how fast or slowly we release our breath. The abdominal muscles relax on the inhalation and gradually engage on the exhalation.
> * Locate your kick-out muscle.
> * Observe that its natural engagement is more like a small contraction rather than a pulling-in or pushing-out.

2. Are you holding your breath?
You must allow your diaphragm free range of movement. Do not prevent it from relaxing completely on the exhalation.
> * Imagine using all of your breath as you sing each phrase.
> * Move your shoulders and hips if you tend to hold your breath.

3. Are you tensing the glottis or tightening your pharynx in order to slow down the release of your breath?
When the subglottic pressure is too intense, the vocal folds and throat tense. The goal is to keep the air pressure lower in the body and allow for a regulated subglottic pressure.
> * Imagine that you are inhaling as you sing.
> * Imagine you are "sitting on your breath" as you sing.

4. Are you feeling strain on higher notes?
Remember, the vocal folds thin and lengthen on the higher pitches. We need to supply enough airflow to vibrate them without overwhelming them. We balance our airflow by simultaneously anchoring our breath.
> * Sing at a softer volume.
> * Free your breath by rolling your shoulders while singing.
> * Keep the air pressure lower in your body.

You've built the Engine!

Congratulations on having completed all of the chapters related to **ENERGY**!

* You have explored your body's alignment and understand the importance of posture.
* You have learned about the respiratory system.
* You have learned how breathing for singing differs from daily breathing.
* You have a deeper understanding of how your breath and breath pressure influences your voice.

In short, you have "built the engine" for your instrument. Great job!

VIBRATION

4

PHONATION

If you have ever had laryngitis, you recognize that our ability to speak and sing has everything to do with our **VOCAL FOLDS** (vocal cords). Our breath may be the engine for our instrument, but our sound begins with the vocal folds in our larynx. **PHONATION** is the process by which our vocal folds make a sound. When our outgoing breath meets resistance at our vocal folds, the **SUBGLOTTIC PRESSURE** vibrates our vocal folds and creates **SOUND WAVES**.

To sing, we must coordinate our outgoing breath with the closing of our **GLOTTIS** and sustain enough breath pressure for the duration of a musical phrase. The **ONSET** or **ATTACK** of the note is the first step in this process. At the onset of the note, timing our outgoing breath with the closure of our glottis is critical. If our timing is consistently off, we overcompensate, which can cause damage to our vocal folds. Our goal is to have a **COORDINATED** or **BALANCED ONSET** (attack), where the air from the lungs meets the glottis just as it is closing, and the vocal folds vibrate immediately. The result is a clear and beautiful tone.

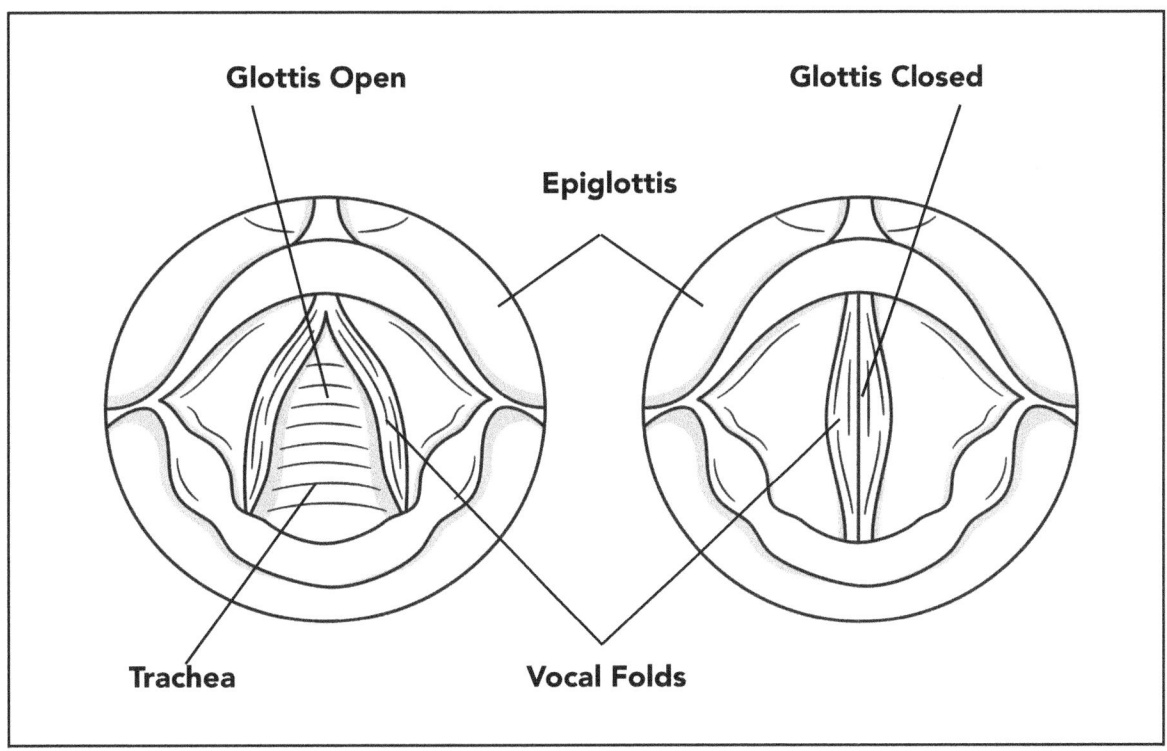

Healthy **PHONATION** requires us to examine the relationship between our energy source (breath) and our vibratory source (vocal folds).

Here's a quick experiment to understand the mechanics involved.

* Say the sentence, "Uncle Eddie eats eggs". [24] Did you notice the glottal "click" at the start of every word? This is a *glottal onset*.
* Speak the same sentence with an "H" at the beginning of every word. "H-Uncle H-Eddie H-eats H-eggs." This is a *breathy onset*.
* Next, speak the sentence and think of the "H" but don't say it.
* Look for the timing where your breath meets your vocal folds just as the glottis closes. This is a *coordinated onset*.
    - Notice that your core muscles engage.
    - This coordination takes practice, so don't give up!

A **GLOTTAL ONSET** is when our glottis closes and our vocal folds connect before our breath releases. If there is a slight delay before the air meets the vocal folds, the breath pressure is more forceful than necessary to vibrate the vocal folds. The result is a glottal "click" at the start of phonation. Glottal tension and possible hoarseness from the over-pressurized attack is the telltale sign of this abrupt onset.

If your habit is tensing your glottis and over-pressurizing your breath, imagine singing on a sigh. This will help you feel the sensation of releasing glottal tension. Although challenging at first, over time, your tendency towards glottal tension will lessen. If you find it difficult to achieve a lighter, breathier sound, try rolling your shoulders and moving your hips while singing. Moving your body releases tension and frees the breath.

Equally unfavorable is a **BREATHY ONSET** where the breath releases before the glottis closes and the vocal folds do not connect properly. This onset prevents the vocal folds from meeting completely, resulting in a leaky or breathy sound, often causing the singer to run out of breath.

If your tendency is to begin phonation with a breathy onset, try singing with more energy to engage your core muscles. Engaging your core muscles naturally closes the glottis.

To achieve a **COORDINATED ONSET**, the start of the note should be smooth and gentle. Picture your vocal tract being open before the sound is made. Then, allow the breath and sound to pass through the open spaces of your throat and mouth.[25] Your core muscles should engage just as your vocal folds connect. Repeat, "Uncle Eddie eats eggs" with an open vocal position and a gentle *caress*[26] of your core muscles as you begin each word. Note that the sound is not sudden or explosive.

Now, let's address how to protect our vocal folds from abuse. Remember, singing should never hurt. When singing properly, one can sing for an extended period with no issues.

Besides illness, the most common reasons we "lose" our voice are:

* postural tension
* over pressurizing
* over inhaling
* screaming or yelling
* coughing
* singing in the wrong range for our voice
* speaking or singing too loudly because of a noisy environment

Our larynx and vocal folds may be small, but they are mighty! It takes excessive abuse to do permanent damage to them. More often, vocal issues such as **NODULES** and **POLYPS** result from habitual misuse because the swollen vocal folds do not have sufficient time to recover.

Nodules are non-cancerous growths that form on the vocal folds, similar to a callus forming on our fingers when we write with a pencil for a long time. Habitual misuse of our voice causes the vocal folds to swell, and over time, the swollen spots harden and form nodules. Polyps are bigger than nodules and are like blisters on our vocal folds. Both nodules and polyps make it difficult for our vocal folds to connect and vibrate.

Some common symptoms of nodules or polyps include:

* hoarseness
* breathiness
* a "rough" voice
* a "scratchy" voice
* pain when vocalizing
* feeling like you have a "lump in your throat"
* difficulty changing pitch

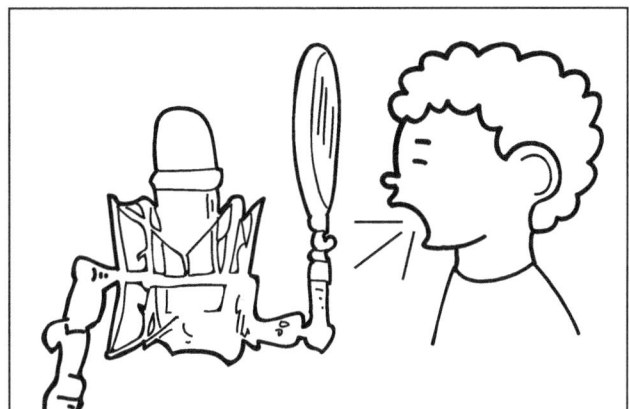

Learning to recognize our behavioral tendencies and the misuse of our voice takes time and self-awareness. Eventually, we learn to change harmful habits and coordinate our onset with ease.

PHONATION EXERCISES

Choose one or two of the following exercises for your daily practice.

Activity #1 PUPPY WHIMPERS
* Whimper like a puppy to coordinate your onset.
* Observe your body's engagement as you find a balanced onset.

Activity #2 MOVE YOUR HEAD!
This exercise can provide a lot of information about where any tensions may be hiding.

* Vocalize while moving your head up and down slowly.
* Vocalize while moving your head from side to side slowly.
* Do your vocal folds remain connected?
* If not, release any tension in your throat and tongue and repeat.

Activity #3 CONNECT THE CORDS!
This exercise familiarizes us with opening and closing our glottis. We sing this exercise on one breath.

* Close your glottis and sing /OO/ for 2 beats.
* Then, open your glottis as you continue singing /OO/ for 2 beats.
* Once again, close your glottis as you continue singing /OO/ for 2 beats.
* Notice your core muscles engage to help your vocal folds reconnect.

Ooo(connect)　　　ooo(breathy)　　　ooo(connect)

Activity #4 FIND IT!
This exercise enhances our glottal awareness. We sing this exercise on one breath.

* Begin by exhaling on an /OO/.
* Then, allow your glottis to close.
* Notice your core muscles must engage during this process.

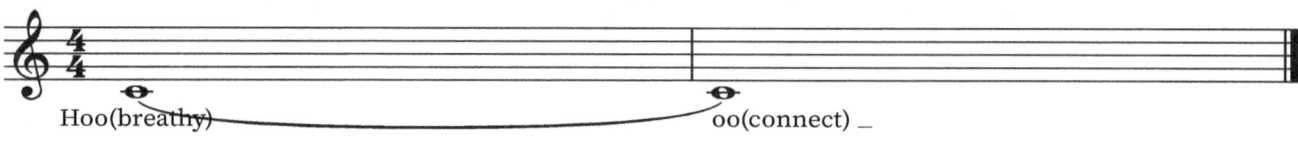

Hoo(breathy)　　　　　　　　oo(connect)

Activity #5 NO MORE SECRETS

* Sing the first part of this exercise with a breathy vocal fold closure.
* Pause and inhale.
* Sing the second part with a connected vocal fold closure.
* Notice your core muscles must engage during this process.

Oo (breathy)   Oo (connect)

REGISTERS

5

REGISTERS

Our voice can express our every thought and idea. When we speak, our vocal folds change length and tension quickly and without conscious awareness. The same mechanics take place when we sing, and they occur as naturally as they do in speech.

Every voice has three distinct areas, which I will refer to as registers. There is the low register or "chest" voice, the medium register or "middle" or "mix" voice, and the high register or "head" voice.[27]

Singers often complain about the inconsistency between their "head" voice and their "chest" voice. You can feel the obvious differences between these two voices when you "He-Haw" like a donkey or yodel on /AH/ like Tarzan!

To understand why there are such obvious differences between our "head" and "chest" voices, picture two rubber bands, one thin and one thick. Imagine stretching them over the top of a glass. If you pluck them and adjust them to make the same pitch, a difference in their tone color is obvious. The thick rubber band would make a more robust sound, like our chest voice, while the thin rubber band would be lighter and less vigorous, like our head voice.[28]

If we stretched the rubber bands further, they would lengthen and become thin. This increase in tension raises their pitch because of the increase in the rate of vibration, or **FREQUENCY**,[29] which is defined as the number of vibration cycles that occur each second within a sound wave. The higher the frequency of a sound wave, the higher the pitch.

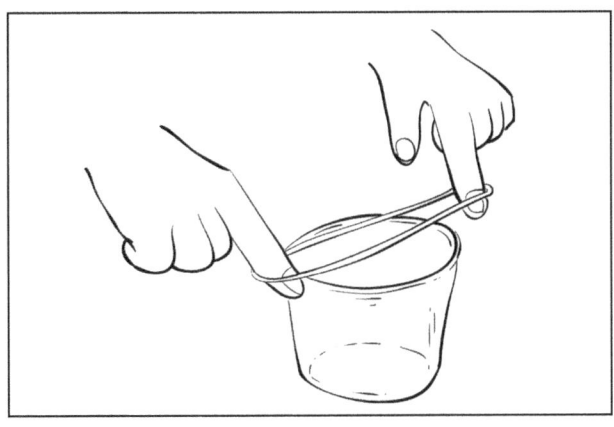

Our vocal folds can change length and width because they attach to the **THYROID CARTILAGE** in the front of our larynx and the **ARYTENOID CARTILAGE** at the back of our larynx. These cartilages rock and glide to change our vocal folds shape by engaging either the **THYROARYTENOID (TA) LIGAMENTS** or **CRICOTHYROID (CT) LIGAMENT**. These ligaments are opposing muscles, meaning one contracts while the other releases and vice versa. One ligament will be more dominant than the other, depending on the note being sung. By recognizing that *both ligaments are always actively opposing one another*, we create a smoother and richer sound as we transition between our registers.

Let's further explore how the **CT LIGAMENT** and **TA LIGAMENTS** affect the voice. Begin by imitating a small puppy whimpering. In this register, your **CT LIGAMENT** dominates and pivots the **THYROID CARTILAGE** forward and down. The **CT LIGAMENT** *(Figure A)* is on the exterior of our larynx. When the **CT LIGAMENT** contracts, the **THYROID CARTILAGE** pivots and rocks forward, causing your vocal folds to lengthen and thin creating a higher pitch. We typically refer to this as our upper register or "head" voice.

Figure A

- Hyoid Bone
- Thyroid Cartilage
- **CT LIGAMENT**
- Cricoid Cartilage

Frontal view of larynx

Figure B

- Arytenoid Cartilages
- **TA LIGAMENT**
- Vocal Folds
- Thyroid Cartilage

Now, imitate Santa with a big HO-HO-HO. In this register, a low voice occurs because our **TA LIGAMENTS** are dominant and your vocal folds shorten and widen. The **TA LIGAMENTS** *(Figure B)* run the entire length of the vocal folds. When they pull the arytenoid cartilages toward the thyroid cartilage, our vocal folds become shorter and thicker. Our sound is fuller, similar to the thick rubber band. We typically refer to it as our lower register or "chest" voice. Much of our vocal practice is learning to transition seamlessly between the low and high registers of our voice.

To further your understanding of the **CT LIGAMENT** and **TA LIGAMENTS** and their affect on your vocal folds, place your finger on the front of your larynx; you are touching the **THYROID CARTILAGE**. Hum from low to high like a siren. Using good breath support, keep your larynx stable and your tongue relaxed. You should feel the Thyroid Cartilage drop forward and down slightly as you siren from low to high because the **CT LIGAMENT** contracts, pulling the front of the Thyroid Cartilage forward and down slightly. This movement is lengthening your vocal folds. Play with this awareness as you explore your low and high registers on the following exercises.

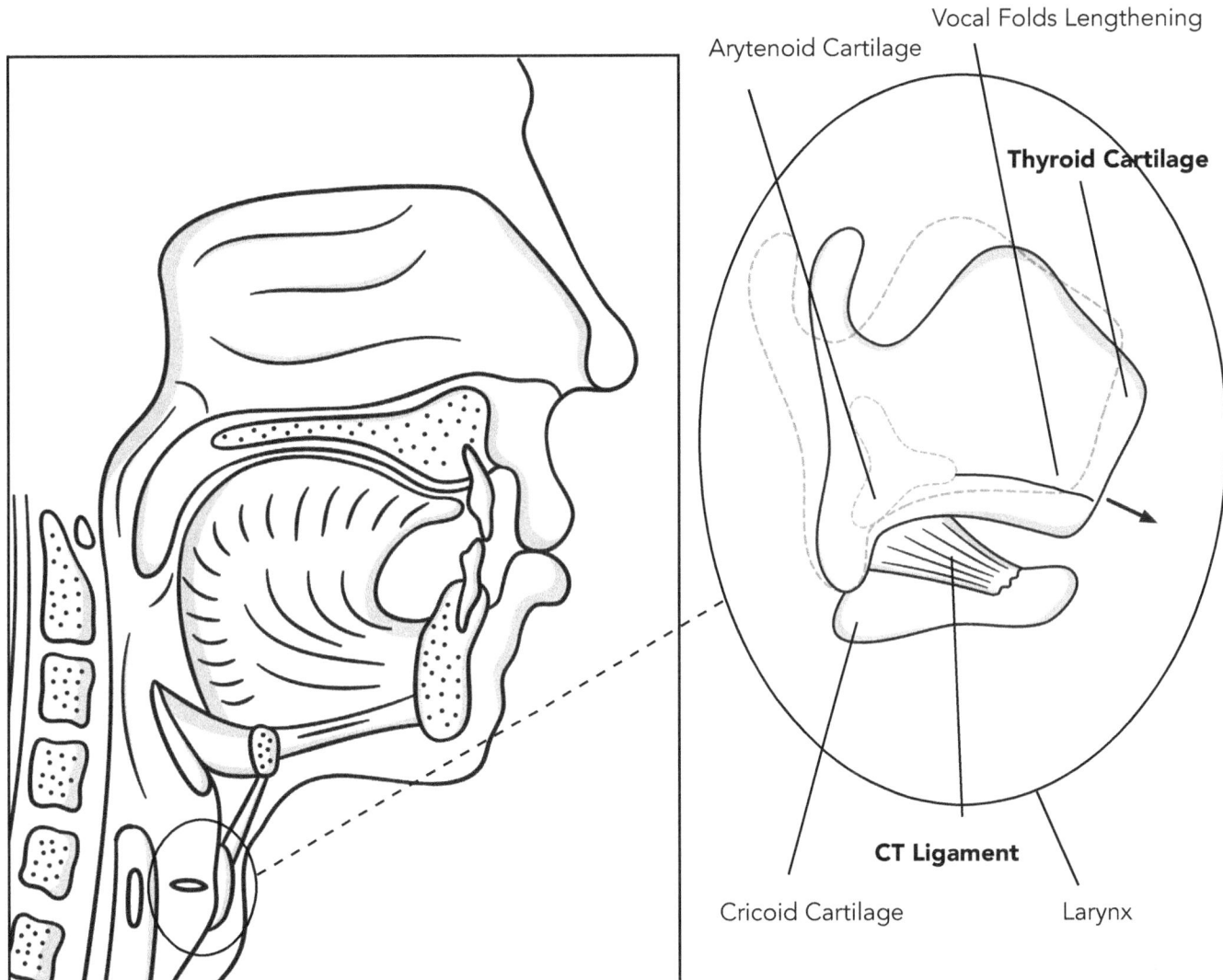

REGISTER EXERCISES

Choose two or three of the following activities for your daily practice.

Activity #6 COUNTING 1, 2, 3
* Count to ten alternating between your low voice and high voice.
* Observe the obvious qualities, sensations, and differences of each register.

Activity #7 THE SNEEZE!
* Pretend you are going to sneeze.
* Say /AH/ in your low voice and /CHOO/ in your high voice.
* Observe the obvious qualities, sensations, and differences of each register.

Activity #8 TALK LIKE A MOUSE
This exercise is helpful when you are having difficulty finding your "head" voice.
* Speak the lyrics to a song in your high voice, like a mouse.
* Using the same high voice, sing the lyrics to that song with the melody.
    - You should be able to feel your "head" voice.

Activity #9 COP CAR!
* "Whoop" like a police siren beginning in your lower register, then moving into your upper register.
* Observe the obvious qualities, sensations, and differences of each register.

Whoop!   Whoop!   Whoop!   Whoop!   Whoop!   Whoop!   Whoop!   Whoop!

6

REGISTER COORDINATION

When we transition from our low voice to our high voice and vice versa, we feel what is commonly called the "**BREAK**", which is actually the physical differences between our "head" and "chest" voices. Ultimately, we want to transition through our "break" seamlessly to form one uniform sound. We do this by learning to coordinate three things: **ENERGY, DEPTH,** and **SPACE** [30] as we sing from the bottom of our voice to the top.

Before we explore each of these elements, understand that the discussion of **REGISTERS** and **REGISTER COORDINATION** can be confusing. As James McKinney writes, "No other area of vocal instruction is as shrouded with mystery, semantic confusion, and controversy as the subject of registers and registration."[31] That said, this is my take on the topic.

First, remember that every voice has three distinct areas: the low register or "chest" voice, the medium register or "middle" voice, and the high register or "head" voice.[32]

In Chapter 5, we learned that the ThyroArytenoid (TA) and CricoThyroid (CT) ligaments are *opposing muscles*. You will recall when the TA ligament contracts, our vocal folds shorten and thicken. This is commonly called our "chest" voice or lower register. Conversely, when our CT ligament contracts, our vocal folds lengthen and thin, resulting in our "head voice" or high register. However, there is never a point at which one muscle takes over from the other completely. Depending on the tone being sung, one muscle will be more dominant than the other, but both are active as we sing.

Our goal is to "mix" or "blend" the qualities of the "chest" and "head" voices throughout our middle register. When we integrate both voices, we are less inclined to carry our chest voice too high, which causes our voice to become strident, and we are less inclined to carry our head voice too low, which causes our voice to become weak.

EXAMPLE USING A TYPICAL FEMALE VOICE

Figure C

In **Figure C**, notice the **F#** is an evenly balanced engagement of the "head" voice and the "chest" voice. Notice the large span where both the "chest" voice and the "head" voice are active and share the responsibilities of pitch production in varying ratios.

Our directional approach will determine the quality of a note. If we approach **F#** from our upper register, it will share more of the "head" voice qualities to blend. If we approach the same **F#** from our lower register, it will share more of the "chest" voice qualities. A common approach when transitioning through our registers is to imagine "lightening up" the quality of our voice as we sing higher and adding more "weight" when we descend.

Working with the concepts of **ENERGY, DEPTH** and **SPACE**[33] activates our physical anatomy and eases the transition through our registers. Let's examine how **ENERGY, DEPTH,** and **SPACE** affect our voice keeping in mind that we are always gauging if we need more *breath flow* or *resistance to the breath flow* as we sing.

As discussed at the beginning of this book, our energy must change depending on the pitch we are singing. We learned that higher notes require more "energy". James McKinney states, "As you sing up a scale, each tone requires a little more energy than the one just below it."[34]

However, there are nuances! Since our vocal folds lengthen and are thin for higher notes, we must be mindful to not use too forceful a breath, as that would interfere with our glottis' ability to close and vibrate our vocal folds easily. **DEPTH** helps us manage our airflow.

Contrary to most people's natural inclination, the higher the note, the deeper or more "anchored" our breath should feel. Since our natural habit is to tighten and lift our larynx on higher notes, we must counter this habit by *deepening* the engagement of our inner abdominal canister to stabilize our diaphragm and regulate our outgoing breath. Picturing our breath "low" in our body helps this process and allows for a richer sound. Our entire body needs to become involved with this process as we imagine a lower center of gravity.

To illustrate the nuances of depth and how our core engages: [35]

* Imagine your friend tosses you a ping-pong ball. It's easy to catch with one hand, right? On a scale of 1 to 10, you may describe your body's effort as a level 1.
* Next, imagine your friend throwing a basketball. You would probably use two hands to catch it. No doubt you would feel more core engagement, maybe a 3 or 4.
* Finally, imagine your friend throwing a bowling ball! You would feel a response deep in your body, and your center of gravity would shift downward. This core engagement may feel like a 7 or even an 8 and would certainly help with those high notes!

However, depth also has another meaning when we sing. It describes a deeper, richer sound with each ascending note. The combination of "depth" being both mental and physical assists in creating the third element, **SPACE**.

We will learn more about our vocal tract in the next section on **RESONANCE**. For now, acknowledge that we need to stabilize our larynx as we transition through our range. This stability creates more space in our vocal tract on higher notes.

Remembering that our vocal folds move horizontally is essential to counteract our innate habit of lifting our larynx for high notes or of "pressing down" our larynx for low notes. To experience the space in your vocal tract, siren up and down on an /OO/ or with lip trills. Keeping your larynx stable, notice how the space in your vocal tract increases incrementally as you siren up. These physical changes are slight, but the cumulative effect is noticeable.

One last thing, sing at 75% of your potential volume to help you understand and experience the coordination of your registers. Singing too loudly makes it difficult to transition through your registers easily. Remember to pay attention to any uncomfortable sensations as you gradually extend your range.

Now it's time to practice with these concepts. Eventually, you will be able to blend your low and high registers seamlessly!

REGISTER COORDINATION EXERCISES

Choose one or two of the following activities for your daily practice.

Activity #10 SIGH
 * Sigh lightly (75%) on an /AH/ beginning in your high register.
 * Allow the breath to carry your voice down to your low register.
 * Repeat several times until you can transition easily.
  - Be aware of "Energy", "Depth" and "Space" as you sing.

Activity #11 SIRENS
 * Keeping the tip of your tongue touching your bottom front teeth, siren up and down on an /OO/.
 * Remember to keep your larynx stable and allow more space in the vocal tract as your voice ascends.
  - Be aware of "Energy", "Depth" and "Space" as you sing.

Activity #12 HIP [36]
 * Engage your "inner abdominal canister" as you transition through your range.
  - Be aware of "Energy", "Depth", and "Space" as you sing.

Activity #13 HEY, TAXI!
This exercise has two parts:
 * #1 Call for a taxi!
 * #2 Use that same energy and sing, "Hey, Taxi!"
  - Be aware of "Energy", "Depth", and "Space" as you sing.

Activity #14 MOM!
This exercise is like "Hey, Taxi!"
* #1 Keep your breath pressure low in your body and call "Hey, Mom".
* #2 Lean into that low breath pressure as you sing "Mom".
  - Be aware of "Energy", "Depth", and "Space" as you sing.

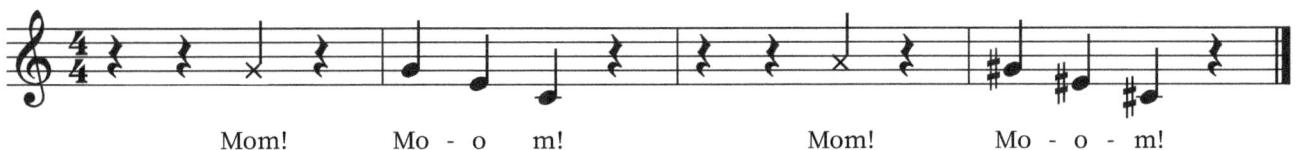

Activity #15 LIGHTEN UP
* Sing on an /OO/ at 75%.
* Repeat with lip trills.
  - Be aware of "Energy", "Depth", and "Space" as you sing.

Activity #16 THE TEASE
* Keep your resonance nasty and nasal as you sing "nya".
  - Be aware of "Energy", "Depth", and "Space" as you sing.

Activity #17 THE DUCK
* Keep your resonance nasty and nasal as you "Quack".
* Observe a widening inside the back of your mouth.
* Try not to let the corners of your mouth widen.
  - Be aware of "Energy", "Depth", and "Space" as you sing.

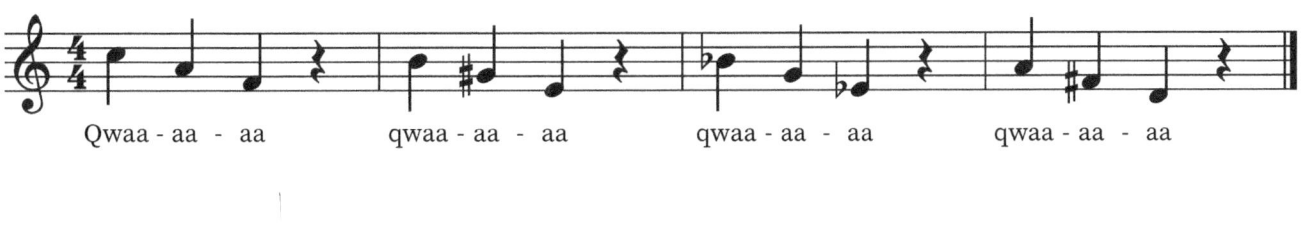

Activity #18 SLOPPY DUCK
* Sing on an /NG/ slurring from note to note.
* Lower the back of your tongue to make the /AH/.
* Repeat and this time lower your tongue to make the /EH/.
    - Be aware of "Energy", "Depth", and "Space" as you sing.

NG - ng - ng - ng - AH - ah   NG - ng - ng - ng - AH - ah

Activity #19 MORNING BRINGS
Transition through your low, middle, and upper registers.
* Sing "**Morning**" in your "chest" voice.
* Sing "**brings the**" in your "chest" voice transitioning to your "middle" voice".
* Sing "**sunny day**" in your "chest" voice transitioning to your "head" voice and then back again to your "chest" voice.
    - Be aware of "Energy", "Depth", and "Space" as you sing.

Morn - ing   brings the   sun - ny   day

Record your own exercises here.

EXERCISES

VIBRATION EXERCISES SUMMARY

PHONATION

    1. PUPPY WHIMPERS   p.40
    2. MOVE YOUR HEAD!   p.40
    3. CONNECT THE CORDS!   p.40
    4. FIND IT!   p.40
    5. NO MORE SECRETS   p.41

REGISTERS

    6. COUNTING 1,2,3   p.46
    7. THE SNEEZE   p.46
    8. TALK LIKE A MOUSE   p.46
    9. COP CAR!   p.46

REGISTER COORDINATION

    10. SIGH   p.50
    11. SIRENS   p.50
    12. HIP   p.50
    13. HEY, TAXI!   p.50
    14. MOM!   p.51
    15. LIGHTEN UP   p.51
    16. THE TEASE   p.51
    17. THE DUCK   p.51
    18. SLOPPY DUCK   p.52
    19. MORNING BRINGS   p.52

VIBRATION REVIEW QUESTIONS

1. Where is the larynx located?
   * In the front of our throat.

2. Where are the vocal folds located?
   * Inside of the larynx.

3. How do vocal folds function when we breathe?
   * The vocal folds separate to allow air into and out of our lungs.

4. How do vocal folds function when we sing?
   * They come together when we speak or sing.

5. What is the glottis?
   * The space between the vocal folds.

6. What are the three ways we can begin the process of phonation? Explain.
   * A BREATHY ONSET is when our breath meets the vocal folds before they connect.
   * A GLOTTAL ONSET is when our vocal folds meet before the release of our breath.
   * A BALANCED ONSET is when the closing of our vocal folds and our breath occur simultaneously. It is what we strive for.

7. What happens to our vocal folds when we sing a high note? Low note?
   * They elongate and get thinner with higher notes.
   * They thicken and shorten with lower notes.

8. What are the two ligaments responsible for thickening or lengthening our vocal folds?
   * The Thyroarytenoid (TA) is dominant in our lower range.
   * The Cricothyroid (CT) is dominant in our upper range.

9. What is "the break"?
   * The obvious differences between the upper and lower registers.

10. What is the "blend" or "mixed" voice?
   * The combination of the upper and lower registers as we transition. This is also called the "middle" register.

11. What are the three elements that should change or "adjust" gradually as we move through our range?
   Energy, space, and depth.

TROUBLESHOOTING

CHAPTER 4 - PHONATION

1. Are you running out of breath? Is your sound "airy"?
 Check that your vocal folds are connecting well.

2. Do you suffer from chronic hoarseness or vocal fatigue?
 This is due to tension. First, check that you are not squeezing and tensing your vocal folds or your larynx.
 Try Moving your shoulders or hips as you sing. This prevents you from "holding" your breath.

CHAPTER 5 - REGISTERS

1. Are you pitchy?
 Most likely, you are unfamiliar with the parameters of your voice. Check if you are bringing your lower register too high or vice versa.
 Sing the pitch or melody in your mind first.
 Make sure you are singing at 75 percent volume.

2. Are you raising your larynx or tightening your throat?
 Check you are not bringing your low register too high.

3. Does your low register sound breathy?
 Check that you are not bringing your high register too low.

CHAPTER 6 - REGISTER COORDINATION

1. Is your throat tightening and your larynx raised?
 Sing at 75% of your volume. This allows an easier transition.

2. Are you too nasal or too throaty?
 Keep the corners of your mouth relaxed and try the "Sloppy Duck" exercise.
 Notice the shape changes inside your mouth and not externally.

VIBRATION

Good Vibrations!

You are making fantastic progress! Having completed the section on our instrument's **VIBRATORY SOURCE**, you now understand how your voice produces sound.

* You have learned about the process of phonation.
* You have learned how the larynx and the vocal folds function.
* You have learned how the length and thickness of our vocal folds determine our pitch.
* You are aware of the differences between our lower register, middle register, and upper register.
* You are learning how to transition through them easily.

Well done! Now you are ready to move on to the final chapters and learn about what makes your instrument unique; the **RESONATING CHAMBER**.

VOCAL TRACT

7

VOCAL TRACT

If a tree falls in the forest, does it make a sound? Before you respond, here is another question. If our vocal folds vibrate, do they make a sound? Would it surprise you to know that they actually make a rather weak, buzzing sound by themselves? So what happens in our **VOCAL TRACT** that changes those buzzing sounds into our unique voice?

Brace yourself. This next section includes a lot of anatomy and physics, but I will attempt to make it easily digestible. To begin, let's understand that sound is energy, just like electricity and light. Every sound, whatever it may be, starts with something vibrating, causing the surrounding air molecules to vibrate and begin a chain reaction of vibrations called **SOUND WAVES**. The sound waves must travel through a medium, such as air or water, to our ears, and then to our brain, where we recognize the sound waves as sound.

When our vocal folds vibrate, they generate sound waves that travel through our vocal tract where the air in the tract shapes and amplifies the sound waves. Think of our vocal tract as a "tube filled with air" where the sound waves **RESONATE** or **RE-SOUND**. Since each of us has a unique vocal tract, each of us has a unique voice.

The entire vocal tract begins at our larynx and includes our throat, tongue, soft palate, jaw, and lips. Unlike the resonating chambers of other instruments, our vocal tract alters size and shape constantly as we sing. This makes our instrument extraordinary and somewhat unwieldy.

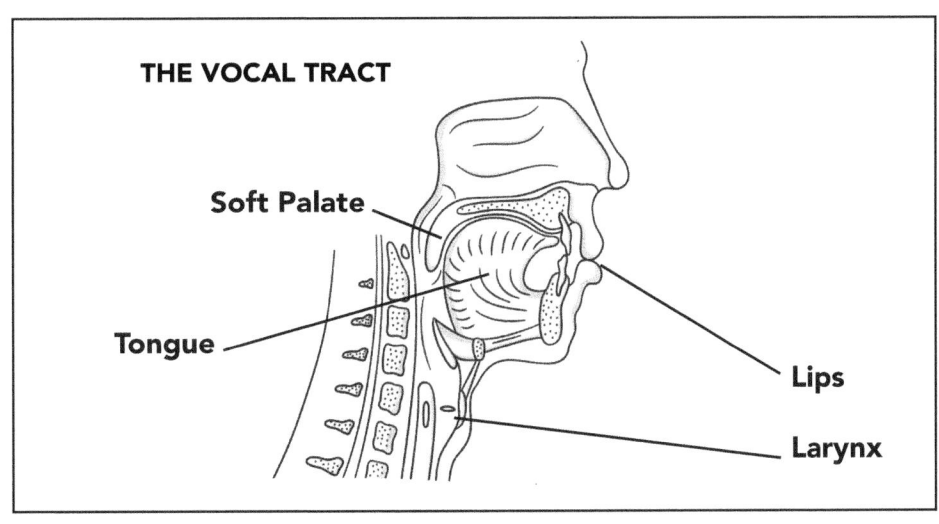

Before we continue, we must acknowledge a basic concept of physics. Sound waves vibrate faster in smaller containers of air, resulting in higher pitches, and they vibrate slower in larger containers of air, resulting in lower pitches. Visualize a tuba and a piccolo and the contrasting sounds they make.

It's helpful to think of our vocal tract as a tube that consists of two separate areas: the space behind the hump of the tongue **(PHARYNX)** and the space in front of the hump of the tongue **(MOUTH CAVITY)**. Tiny physical alterations result in huge acoustical differences. By considering each area of our vocal tract separately, we can adjust any changes with much more specificity.[37]

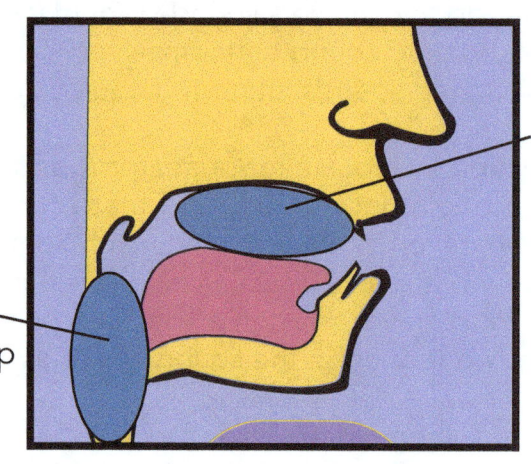

CONTAINER 2 is the air from the hump of the tongue to the lips.

CONTAINER 1 is the air from the larynx to the hump of the tongue.

Let's explore what happens to our sound as we play with the size of each container.[38]

Make **CONTAINER 1 smaller and CONTAINER 2 larger**:

> * Drop your jaw and move your molars apart.
>   - In this position, our throat cavity is smaller and our mouth cavity is larger.
> * Hum on any pitch and **observe the darker quality** of your voice.

Now, let's make **CONTAINER 1 larger and CONTAINER 2 smaller:**

> * Bring your molars together.
>   - In this position, our throat cavity is elongated and our mouth cavity is smaller.
> * Hum on an pitch and **observe the brighter quality** of our voice.

The above are both extreme positions. To find a more balanced sound:

> * Hum on a comfortable pitch.
> * Slowly bring your teeth together and apart, as if you are chewing.

* Continue humming while moving the back of your tongue up towards the roof of your mouth.
* Now bring the back of your tongue down towards the bottom molars.
* Observe how the sound changes as the space in each area of your vocal tract changes.
* Look for a balanced vibration in your mouth, cheeks, and soft palate.

Let's further explore each area of our vocal tract, beginning with **CONTAINER 1**, our throat, or **PHARYNX** which extends from our larynx to the back of our tongue. The pharynx consists of three large bands of constrictor muscles: the **LARYNGOPHARYNX**, the **OROPHARYNX**, and the **NASOPHARYNX**. These muscles are familiar because they engage when we swallow and yawn.

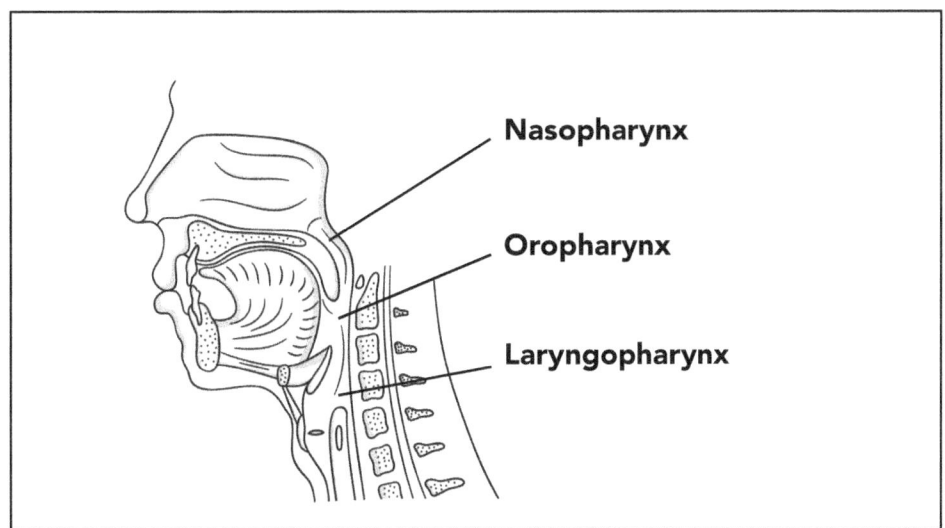

To relax and stabilize our pharynx, we must learn to balance our swallowing and yawning reflexes. To understand how strong the muscles of the pharynx are, place your hand on your throat and swallow. You will feel your larynx and tongue lift as your throat constricts. Now, yawn and notice how the pharynx widens and our larynx lowers. If you feel a powerful sensation in your throat when singing, you may be "swallowing" or "yawning" and must learn to relax the muscles of your pharynx.

Singers often describe a relaxed pharynx feeling as if they are "doing nothing" or the pharynx is "empty". We can feel a relaxed pharynx when we make a small smile or begin a smirk. Another image that helps us experience an open pharynx is to imagine drinking air from a cup and notice the sense of release behind the tongue.

This brings us to the second part of our vocal tract, **CONTAINER 2**, our mouth cavity, which runs from the root of our tongue to our lips. This area includes all the **ARTICULATORS**: our tongue, jaw, soft palate, and lips.

THE TONGUE

Our tongue has a tremendous impact on our vocal tract. Our larynx suspends from the **HYOID BONE**. Also attached to the **HYOID BONE** is the root of our tongue and several jaw and neck muscles. Place your fingers on your larynx and say, "G-G-G" to feel the effects of your tongue's movement on your larynx. Often, vocal issues can trace back to tongue tension because of the tongue's proximity to the larynx and their mutual attachment to the **HYOID BONE**.

Learning how to keep your tongue relaxed, yet available to articulate, takes practice. Try the following tongue explorations to acquaint yourself with this sensation. The goal is to keep your tongue heavy at the root while still allowing the tip of your tongue freedom to move.

* Imagine your tongue is like wall-to-wall carpeting; the front and sides of your tongue touch your lower teeth.
* Now, imagine there is a tiny weight attached to the root of your tongue.
* Take a moment to feel the heaviness in the back of your tongue.
* You may notice that your jaw also releases.
    - This is how a relaxed tongue feels.
* Say "la-la-la" moving just the tip of your tongue.
* Imagine a dollop of honey on the back of your tongue.
    - Be careful not to swallow the honey!

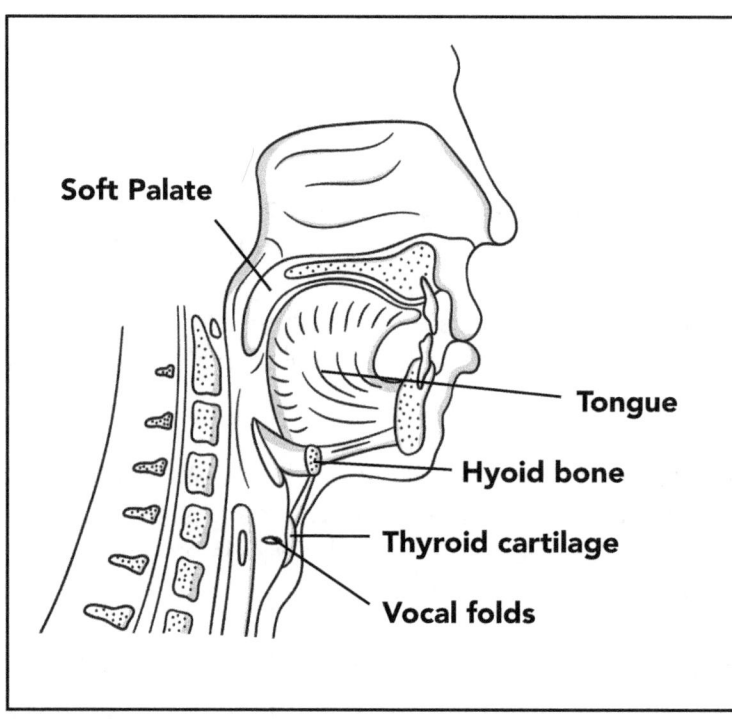

THE JAW

Think about the power it takes to chew something hard or tough. The muscles that open and close our jaws are incredibly strong! These same muscles can become tense, which negatively affects our vocal tract. Our goal is to be aware of our jaw muscles and learn to release them when singing.

To familiarize yourself with a released jaw:

* Place your fingers in front of your ears where your upper and lower jaws hinge.
    - You should feel a slight indentation.
* Allow your jaw to hang open without forcing it open!
* Make small circles with two fingers and massage this area as you keep your jaw heavy.
    - You should feel your jaw muscles release.
    - You should feel your tongue release.

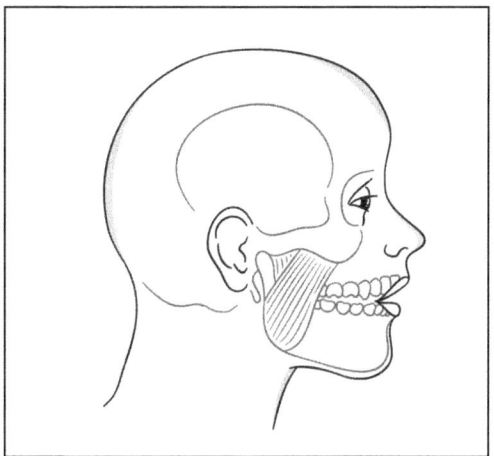

Ideally, we want a relaxed jaw when opening our mouth, but sometimes we notice our jaws thrust forward when we sing. A common cause for this forward thrust is when we bring our lower register too high. If you notice your jaw is in a forward position, try "lightening up" your voice and sing at 75% of your volume. This will allow your TA and CT muscles to coordinate and help you transition from your chest voice to your head voice. Another reason your jaw thrusts forward could be tongue tension, so remind yourself to create the heavy feeling at the root of your tongue.

When I was a young singer, my weekly lessons included working on releasing my jaw. Every week my voice teacher would help me relax my jaw, only to have it just as tense the next week. One day, I was feeling quite frustrated after my lesson. I was deep in thought as I waited for the subway when, suddenly, I realized I was chewing the inside of my mouth! Aha!!! This daily habit was contributing to my jaw tension, and I had to eliminate it!

So, I replaced my bad habit with a positive one. Every time I stopped at a red light or stop sign, I let my jaw go slack and my tongue go heavy. Over time and with practice, I could release my jaw tension on command. Of course, I also avoided habits that created tension such as chewing gum, grinding my teeth, and biting the inside of my mouth! We often have a hard time recognizing how our daily habits affect our voice negatively. If you have chronic vocal issues, begin by looking at your daily habits.

THE SOFT PALATE

The soft palate is important because it is a portal to the nasal cavity or nasopharynx. First, let us locate it! Slide the tip of your tongue along the roof of your mouth. Notice that your palate is hard in the mouth's front and soft in the back. The soft, spongy area in the back is the soft palate. We are most familiar with the soft palate as the area that "stretches" when we yawn. Make a /K/ sound to identify it.

There are several muscles involved with raising and lowering our soft palate. The same muscles that raise our soft palate can also raise our larynx. The muscles that lower our soft palate often accompany lowering and flattening our tongue, which makes isolating the soft palate and its movement challenging.

We achieve optimal resonance when we raise the soft palate, and our sound resonates in the pharynx and mouth cavity. However, when we lower the soft palate, our sound resonates in the nasal cavity, which is not an optimal resonator. Sending our sound through our nasal cavity with a lowered soft palate actually dampens our sound.

Here are some simple tools to help you understand how to shape your soft palate and keep your tongue and soft palate relaxed for optimal resonance while singing.

* Use "the beginning of a yawn" to find the soft palate's ideal shape.
    - This helps raise the soft palate while not tensing it. However, making a full yawn is problematic because it can lower our larynx, so be careful to use just "the beginning of a yawn".
* Think a happy thought and smile to yourself as you inhale.
    - Notice that your soft palate gently lifts.
* Pretend you have a small ball or egg in the back of your throat.
    - This will keep your soft palate slightly raised.

THE LIPS

The last portion of the vocal tract is the **LIPS.** The lips extend or shorten the vocal tract. To keep your lips free of unnecessary tension, imagine them as two rubber tubes that can bounce apart as you sing. Keep your lips soft and rounded.

It is important to be aware of the general shape of your mouth. A helpful image is to picture your mouth as a compass rose that opens North and South but not West and East. This is helpful if your tendency is to widen the corners of your mouth when singing.

Now it's time to put some of this knowledge into practice! Be aware of each exercise's purpose as you practice.

VOCAL TRACT EXERCISES

Choose two or three of the following exercises for your daily practice.

ACTIVITIES #1 - 10 PREPARE THE VOCAL TRACT FOR SINGING

Activity #1 TONGUE MASSAGE
* Hold your jaw in place with your hands.
* Use your thumbs to massage under your chin.
    - This area is your tongue

Activity #2 HOLD YOUR TONGUE
* Stick out your tongue.
* Gently hold your tongue between your teeth.
* Keep your tongue fat and relaxed.
* Siren high and low on /M/ in this position.

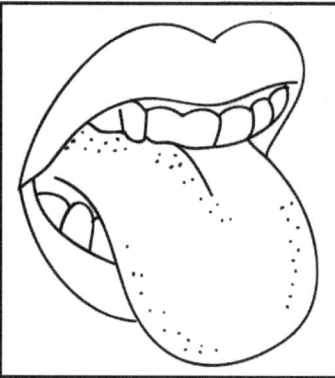

Activity #3 LITERALLY, HOLD YOUR TONGUE
* Use a tissue to hold the tip of your tongue.
* Pull your tongue gently and allow the root of your tongue to release.

Activity #4 TONGUE PRESSES [39]
* Keep the tip of your tongue in contact with your bottom front teeth.
* Make a rocking motion with your tongue by pressing the back of your tongue forward and releasing it repeatedly.
* Say Huh-Yuh-Yuh-Yuh as you rock your tongue forward and back.

Activity #5 MOVE YOUR HEAD
This exercise helps release tension in your vocal tract.
* Move your head up and down slowly as you vocalize.
* Move your head side to side as you vocalize.

Activity #6 JAW STRETCH
* Look up and push your lower jaw forward as if you have an under-bite.
* Hold this position for 5 seconds and then release.
* Bring your head back to normal and balance your skull at the A-O joint.

Activity #7 NECK STRETCH
* Turn your head towards the right and lookup.
* Push your lower jaw forward as if you have an under-bite.
* Hold this position for 5 seconds and then release.
* Bring your head back to normal and balance your skull at the A-O joint.
* Repeat the stretch on the left side.

Activity #8 OPEN THE BOX
This exercise takes time but it is well worth it. It is imperative that your hands alone move your jaw to open and close your mouth and not your jaw muscles!

* Begin with your chin towards your chest.
* Hold your chin with both hands.
* Keep your jaw muscles relaxed as you lift just the top of your head like a box top.
* Next, use your hands to push your lower jaw up in order to close your mouth.
* Repeat this movement until you no longer can.
* Then, reverse direction.
* With your hands in charge, pull down the lower jaw and stabilize it while the upper jaw lowers to meet it.
* Repeat this movement until you no longer can and your chin, once again, is towards your chest.

Activity #9 SING WITH YOUR TONGUE OUT
* Stick your tongue out, keeping it fat and relaxed.
* Sing a song with your tongue in this position.
* Do your best to articulate your lyrics clearly!
* Next, sing the song normally.
    - Notice the root of your tongue is more relaxed, and there is less tension.

Activity #10 TONGUE TWISTERS [39]
Repeat all tongue twisters several times. (START SLOWLY)

A. BUH - DUH - GUH - DUH
B. PUH - TUH - KUH - TUH
C. TOPEKA BODEGA
D. RED LEATHER, YELLOW LEATHER, LAVENDER LEATHER, TOO!

ACTIVITIES #11 - #31 FOCUS ON ALL AREAS OF THE VOCAL TRACT.

Activity #11 ONE NOTE HUM
   * Listen for the changes in your resonance as you move through this exercise.

Activity #12 HEY-YA!
   * Keep your tongue in contact with your bottom teeth and try not to move your jaw!

Activity #13 TONGUE INDEPENDENCE
   * Hold your chin and keep the tip of your tongue in contact with your bottom front teeth.
   * Keep your chin still and move just your tongue as you sing.

Activity #14 YUM-YUM
You can also sing this exercise on /YA/.

   * Keep the tip of your tongue in contact with your bottom front teeth.
   * Maintain a relaxed throat and mimic chewing as you sing on YUM.

Activity #15 NG-AH
This exercise helps identify all the areas of the pharynx.

* Keep your tongue in contact with your bottom front teeth.
* Make the /NG/ sound by exhaling a tiny puff of air through your nose while you touch the back of your tongue to the soft palate.
* Move just the root of your tongue down to make the /AH/ sound.

NG AH NG AH NG AH NG AH   NG_ AH_   NG AH NG AH NG AH NG AH   NG_ AH_

Activity #16 MAY-A
* Keep the root of your tongue heavy.
* Stabilize your larynx as you sing.

May-a may-a may-a may-a   may_ a   May-a may-a may-a may-a   may_____

Activity #17 SU-LU
* Keep the root of your tongue heavy.
* Stabilize your larynx as you sing.
* Keep your lips relaxed as they extend to form the /U/ sound.

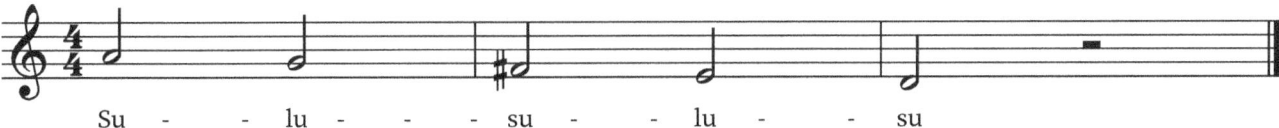

Su - lu - - su - lu - - su

Activity #18 DUH!
* Imagine your tongue and jaw are numb from novocaine.
* Keep your jaw heavy and hanging as you sing.

Duh__   Duh__   Duh____   Duh__   Duh__   Duh_____

Activity #19 KANA
This exercise loosens the tongue.

* Imagine your jaw and tongue are numb from novocaine.
* Let your jaw hang; the root of your tongue feels heavy.
* Isolate your tongue as you sing.
    - Do not move your jaw!

Activity #20 TONGUE RELEASE
You can also sing this exercise on /L/ or /N/.

* Keep your tongue fat and the root heavy.
* Locate the hard ridge above your top front teeth.
* Touch the tip of your tongue to this hard palate ridge behind your top teeth.
* Keep your jaw slack and your larynx stable as you sing.
    - Don't forget to engage your breath support!

Activity #21 LI-LO
* Imagine your jaw and tongue are numb from novocaine.
* Let your jaw hang; the root of your tongue feels heavy.
* Isolate your tongue as you sing.
* Keep your jaw heavy and hanging.

Activity #22 RED LEATHER, YELLOW LEATHER, BLUE LEATHER
* Maintain optimal space in your mouth and pharynx as you articulate.

Activity #23 LA-GA
* Keep your jaw heavy and hanging.
* Keep the root of your tongue fat and lazy.
* Isolate your tongue as you sing this exercise!

la-ga la-ga la-ga la-ga   la-ga la-ga la-ga la-ga   la-ga la-ga la-ga la-ga   Lo

Activity #24 LOUIE!
* Keep your jaw heavy and hanging.
* Keep the root of your tongue fat and lazy.
* Maintain a stable vocal tract as you articulate.
* Sing lightly and with speed.

Louie   louie   louie   louie   louie   louie   louie   louie   louie!

Activity #25 "K" STUTTER [41]
Sing this exercise with a hard "G" as well.

* Keep the tip of your tongue in contact with the bottom front teeth.
* Keep your jaw heavy and hanging.
* Isolate your tongue to make the /K/ sound.
* Keep your jaw still!

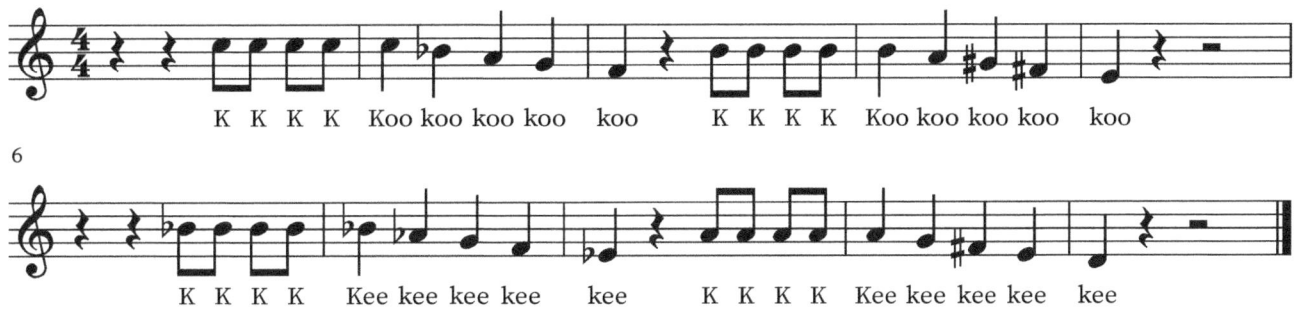

K K K K Koo koo koo koo koo   K K K K Koo koo koo koo koo

K K K K Kee kee kee kee kee   K K K K Kee kee kee kee kee

Activity #26 BOI
Bounce your lips and keep your tongue fat and lazy.

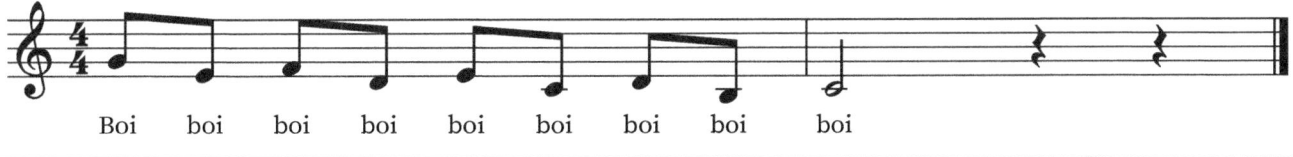

Boi boi boi boi boi boi boi boi boi

Activity #27 KITTELY KIT
This articulation exercise loosens our tongue.

* Maintain a heavy root of the tongue.
* Isolate the tip of your tongue as you articulate a crisp /T/ sound.
    - Be mindful that you do not tense your jaw.

Kittely kittely kittely kittely   kit   Kittely kittely kittely kittely   kit

Activity #28 BI-GI-DI
* Keep your jaw heavy and hanging.
* Imagine your lips are rubber.
* Keep the root of your tongue fat and lazy.
* Maintain a stable vocal tract as you articulate.
* Sing lightly and with speed.

Bi-gi-di   Pi-gi-di   Bi-gi-di   Pi-gi-di   Bi-g-di Pi-gi-di Bi-gi-di Pi-gi-di Bop!

Activity #29 LAZY BABY
* Imagine your lips are rubber.
* Keep the root of your tongue fat and lazy.
* Maintain a stable vocal tract as you articulate.
* Sing lightly and with speed as you "bounce" your lips.

Beh   beh   beh   beh   beh   beh   beh _   Beh   beh   beh   beh   beh _

Activity #30 MA-OH

In this exercise we are looking for stability in the pharynx and mouth as we move from /MA/ to /OH/.

* Keep your jaw heavy and hanging.
* Imagine your lips are rubber.
* Keep the root of your tongue fat and lazy.
* Maintain a stable vocal tract as you articulate.
* Sing lightly and with speed.

Ma-oh ma-oh ma-oh ma - oh   Ma-oh ma-oh ma-oh ma - oh   Ma-oh

Activity #31 MELLOW

* Maintain a heavy jaw and root of the tongue.
* Isolate your tongue as you articulate.
* Maintain a stable vocal tract as you sing.

mel - low   mel - low   mel - low   mel - low   mel - low

8

SOVT (SEMI OCCLUDED VOCAL TRACT)

SEMI-OCCLUDED VOCAL TRACT (SOVT) or partially closed vocal tract training is a healthy way to warm up and cool down our voice. With SOVT training, we are creating the opportunity for our vocal folds to vibrate easily with exercises like lip trills, tongue trills, humming, and singing through straws!

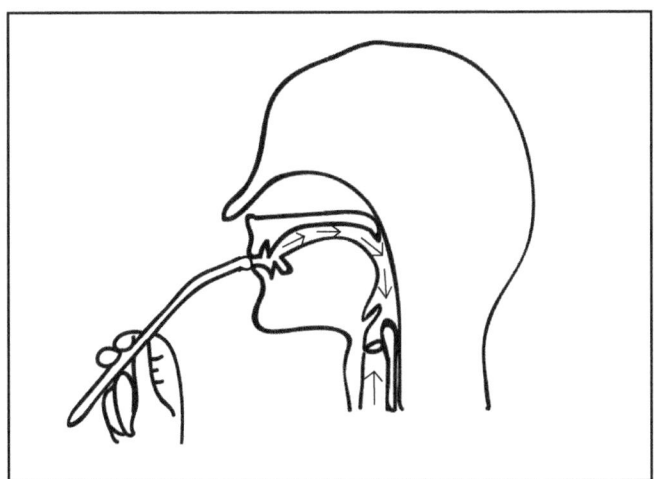

Here's how it works. In Chapter 4, we learned that when the breath pressure from our lungs meets resistance at our vocal folds, the subglottic pressure vibrates the vocal folds and creates sound waves. With a semi-occluded vocal tract, our mouth is partially closed, and it reflects the outgoing acoustic energy back towards the vocal folds, vibrating them from above. When the breath pressure from the lungs and the "back" pressure from the lips are in balance, the vocal folds can vibrate most efficiently. Exploring our range becomes safe and comfortable because there is more energy and less strain on our vocal folds. [42]

Irene and Harris write, "Straw Phonation can be compared to doing exercises in a pool. There is less impact and stress on the muscles while still allowing them to stretch." [43]

There are many vocal issues that **SOVT** warm-ups and cool-downs can remedy. The most common issues are a disconnected sound, vocal fatigue, vocal "heaviness", and the dreaded vocal "break".

The renowned voice scientist, Ingo R. Titze, helped pioneer this important singer's tool. In his work, Titze uses the straw as a training and rehabilitation tool. "Because there is so much back pressure happening it makes it so you cannot over squeeze." [44] The result is a lower larynx and a widening effect on our airway.

Titze explains how vocalizing through a straw "unpresses" the vocal folds.

His demonstration begins with pitch glides.
       * Starting with your lowest note, glide up to your highest note.
          - He recommends doing this 1 -2 minutes.
       * Next, he describes making "hills" or accents through your straw.
          - I liken this to "revving an engine" with small abdominal pulses.
       * Progressively, make larger accents or "hills".
       * Finally, he encourages choosing a song and vocalizing it through your straw.
          - He demonstrates this with the National Anthem because the melody covers a wide range and there are many opportunities to sing using energy accents.

Remember, while the mouth area is partially closed or closed completely, the rest of your vocal tract is open. Begin with pitch glides through the straw and graduate to lip trills, humming and singing on an /OO/. It is important to always use good breath support and not engage your throat as you explore your range.

Try doing SOVT exercises 2 - 3 minutes daily for significant results. Make this the first exercise of the day, the last exercise of the day, or a reset for your voice on days when you have heavy vocal activity.

SOVT EXERCISES

Choose one or two of the following activities for your daily practice.

Activity #32 STRAW SIRENS
Make sure no air escapes through your nose or around your lips. Double-check by holding your nose as you sing.

* Using a straw, siren up and down from low to high.
* Repeat for one minute.
* Next, make smaller pitch glides or "hills" progressively using good support.
* Repeat for one minute.

Activity #33 LIP TRILLS
* Blow air through you lips.
* Add a pitch as you blow the air through your lips.
* Think 'UH' to help keep your vocal tract open and your tongue relaxed.
    - Place your fingers on the corners of your mouth if you find lip trills difficult and keep practicing!

Oo - - - Oo   Oo - - - Oo

Activity #34 STRAW BUBBLES
This is an excellent tool to gauge if you are forcing or "over blowing" your breath.

* Place one end of a straw in a glass of water.
* Siren on /OO/.

Oo - - - Oo   Oo - - - Oo

Activity #35 STRAW VOWELS
* Sing all the vowels through a straw.

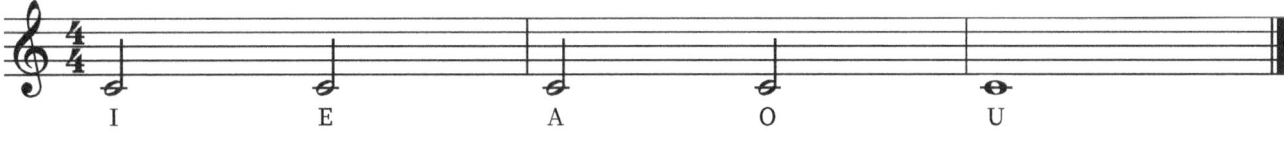

I   E   A   O   U

Activity #36 SING A SONG
* Sing the lyrics of a song through the straw.

Activity #37 VIBRATE THE ARTICULATORS
* Vocalize with /Z/, /ZH/, /V/, /M/, /N/, /NG/.

Oo - - - Oo   Oo - - - Oo

Activity #38 OCTAVE PLUS
This exercise can also be sung with *lip trills*.

* Using a straw, glide your pitch through the melody.
* Keep this light and slurry as you sing /O/.
* Think "UH" as you sing to release your pharynx.

Oo - oo - oo - oo - oo - oo - oo - oo - oo - oo - oo - oo - oo

Activity #39 SLOPPY DUCK
* Keep the tip of your tongue in contact with your front bottom teeth.
* Gently blow a little puff of air through your nostrils just before you vocalize on /NG/.
* Sing with a very connected and lazy sound.

NG - - - AH - - - NG - - - AH - - -

Activity #40 NG SLIDES
* Keep the tip of your tongue in contact with the bottom teeth.
* Gently blow a little puff of air through your nostrils just before you vocalize on /NG/.
* Sing with a very connected and lazy sound.
* Engage your support muscles.

NG _____ AH _____ NG _____ AH _____

9

VOWELS

Just as a sculptor molds and changes the shape of a piece of clay, we master the shaping of our vocal tract to mold and shape our vowels. Although singing is a combination of vowels and consonants, the vowel sustains and carries the sound and forms the basis of a beautiful tone.

Let's begin with the five Italian vowels, which are often the first set of vowels we learn to sing:

[i] ee, [e] eh, [a] ah, [o] oh, [u] oo

These vowels are referred to as pure vowels or **MONOPHTHONGS** because the tongue and lips remain relatively stationary as we sing them. Essentially, the vocal tract does not move mid-vowel. A simple way to remember their proper pronunciation is to think of the following colors.[45]

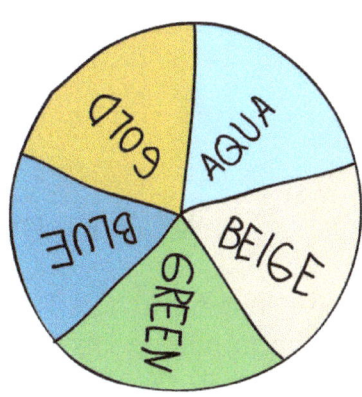

[i]	GREEN
[e]	BEIGE
[a]	AQUA
[o]	GOLD
[u]	BLUE

Although singing exercises tend to focus on the five Italian vowels, I suggest becoming familiar with the other seven monophthongs that are a part of speech. After all, we can't sing lyrics without them!

[ɪ]	WITH, BILL TIN
[ʊ]	PUT, LOOK, GOOD
[ə]	THE, US, CUT
[æ]	ASK, BAT, HAVE
[ɝ]	WORD, BURN, HER
[ɔ]	ALL, CHALK, JAW

Besides monophthongs, we have **DIPHTHONGS**, or gliding vowels, which are words that have two vowel sounds making up a single syllable. In our daily speech, words with diphthongs have a short "on glide" and a longer "off glide". However, when singing diphthongs, we do the opposite and extend the first vowel sound before quickly ending with the second vowel sound. Speak the words *mind, loud,* and *coin* normally. Notice the short "on glide" and longer "off glide". Now, try speaking the words with a longer "on glide" and shortened "off glide". The latter is how we pronounce diphthongs when singing.

<u>SPEECH</u>

		Short + long	**Short + long**
Mind	=	Ma + ind	[a] + [i]
Loud	=	La + ud	[a] + [u]
Coin	=	Co + in	[o] + [i]

<u>SINGING</u>

		Long + Short	**Long + Short**
Mind	=	Ma + ind	[a] + [i]
Loud	=	La + ud	[a] + [u]
Coin	=	Co + in	[o] + [i]

VOWEL RESONANCE

Did you know every vowel has a pitch?[46] That's right! Speak each vowel without actually vocalizing as you flick your fingernail against the side of your larynx. Can you hear the different pitches as you form each vowel? (WARNING: BE GENTLE!) Our vocal tract changes its size and shape with each vowel creating each vowel's unique set of frequencies.

Think of each vowel as having its own acoustical parameter or "fingerprint".[47] Our goal as singers is to target each vowel's pitch center to achieve maximum clarity and resonance. The farther we go from the center or "bullseye", the muddier or more indistinguishable the vowel becomes.

Let me explain. Imagine you are listening to the radio, and you are hearing a station, but there is some static. You slowly turn the dial, tuning into the radio station until you can hear the station's frequencies "loud and clear". We must do the same with every vowel. Depending on the pitch, register, and volume of the note being sung, we must form each vowel's optimal shape with our vocal tract. In doing so, we are enhancing each vowel's ability to resonate and "ring" clearly.

So, how do we find the pitch center of each vowel? Let's begin by remembering that small physical changes can make huge acoustical differences.

Depending on the tongue's position, vowels are categorized as either front, back, or central. In front vowels, the body or "hump" of the tongue arches towards the front of the mouth. In back vowels, the body of the tongue arches towards the back of the mouth. In central vowels, the body of the tongue arches towards the center of the mouth.

Notice the small adjustments to your tongue and all of your articulators as you say the words below. You will be transitioning from a closed mouth position to an open mouth position and vice versa. Observe the bright or dark qualities of each vowel as the position of your tongue shifts.

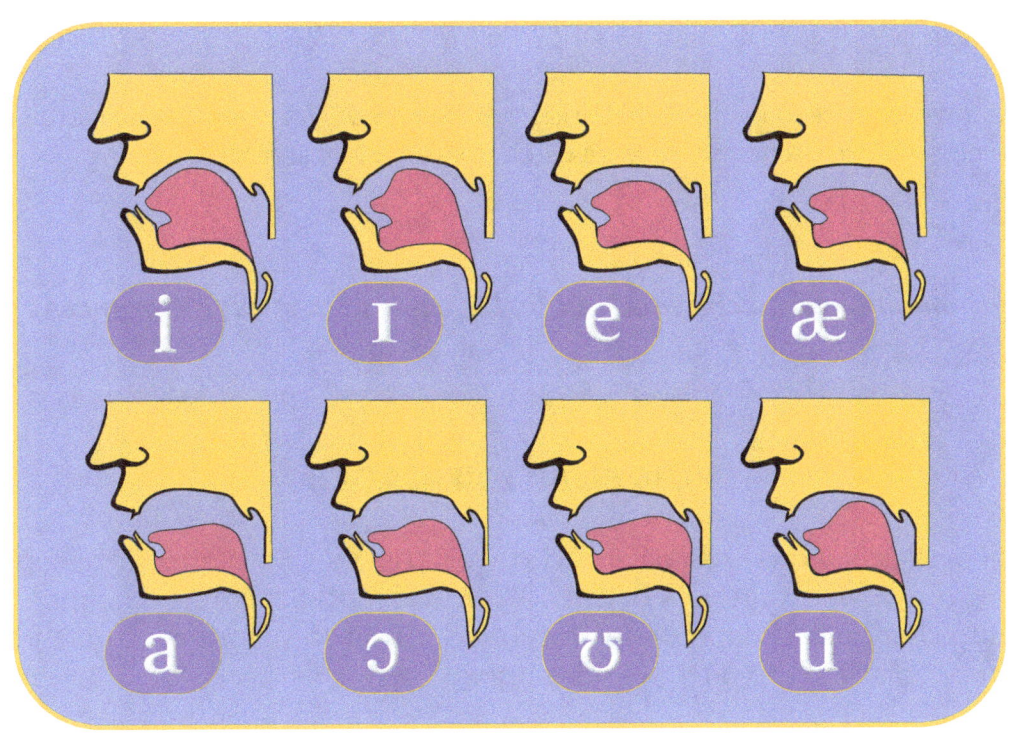

FRONT VOWELS

CLOSED (Narrow)   OPEN (Wide)

[i] heed   **[ɪ] hid**   **[e] head**   **[æ] had**

BACK VOWELS

OPEN (Wide)   CLOSED (Narrow)

[a] hod   **[ɔ] hawed**   **[ʊ] hood**   **[u] who'd**

Each vowel sound is determined by the size and shape of the mouth cavity. Let's try the following exploration to further illustrate this point.

* Sing [a] and slowly press the tip of your tongue against your bottom teeth.
* Allow the root of your tongue to move forward.
    - Note how this tongue position changes the quality of the [a] vowel.
* Next raise the "hump" of your tongue towards the roof of your mouth.
    - Note how this tongue position alters the [a] vowel.
* Now rest your tongue in the bottom of your mouth and purse your lips as you sing [a].
* Widen the corners of your mouth as you sing [a].
* Narrow your lips as you sing [a].
    - Again, note how these changes effect the quality of the [a] vowel.
* Continue moving your articulators until your mouth position offers the most clarity and ease.

To find the center of each vowel requires us to experiment. Try the above exercise with all the vowels. The closer you are to the vowel's pitch center, the easier it is to sing!

Small physical changes can make huge acoustical differences.

VOWEL MODIFICATION

We often refer to pure vowels as balanced vowels. As we sing higher, it becomes more difficult to keep our vowels pure or "balanced". Vowel modification is when we allow subtle adjustments to change the shape of our vocal tract. This allows for the vowel's frequencies to be more compatible with the pitch we are singing.

To gain a better understanding of how vowel modification works, sing [a] and *slowly* glide your voice up an octave. Do not allow any movement or adjustments in your mouth cavity or pharynx. This includes your soft palate and tongue! Did you find it challenging? No doubt the sound was not what you expected as you ascended the octave! Since we did not allow any alterations to our vocal tract, our [a] was less resonant and difficult to sing.

Now, siren up the octave on [a] again, but this time allow changes to naturally take place in your vocal tract. You may have noticed that as you sang higher, your pharynx and tongue adjusted their position to unify your sound. How we sing the [a] vowel in our lower voice differs from the way we sing the [a] vowel in our upper voice. As our vocal folds change length and width, our pharynx, tongue, and jaw adjust in response. Our register (*"chest voice"*, *"middle voice"*, *"head voice"*) determines the length and width of our vocal folds which, in turn, influences our vocal tract.

A "DEEPER DIVE"

Further exploration of vowels requires a brief lesson in **ACOUSTICS,** which leads us to **FORMANTS** and **HARMONICS**. In order to produce our voice's resonance, power, timbre, intelligibility, and unique qualities, the subtle adjustments we make to our vocal tract when we "tune" our vowels are necessary so that the formants and the harmonics can synchronize.

Here's how it works. When we sing a tone, we are really producing a complex sound made up of multiple **FREQUENCIES** called **HARMONICS**. You can see from the chart below that every tone has many frequencies vibrating at the same time that occur at multiple intervals.

HARMONIC-OVERTONE SERIES

The lowest harmonic is the strongest and loudest frequency. We call it the **FUNDAMENTAL FREQUENCY** and perceive it as the pitch. Stacked above the fundamental frequency is the second harmonic frequency, third harmonic frequency, and so on making up one complete set of harmonic frequencies. Every time we change the spacing in our mouth and pharynx, it affects the harmonics produced by our vocal folds.

As the harmonic frequencies travel through our vocal tract, some become louder and some become softer, depending on our vocal tract's unique length and shape. The frequencies that become stronger than average are called **FORMANTS**. Think of formants as louder energy boosts that alter the original sound and give our voice its unique tonal quality.

Harmonics are produced by the vocal folds. Formants are produced by the vocal tract.

Malformed vowels create a clash between the formant frequencies and the harmonic frequencies, making them incompatible. When this happens, there is a lot of "static". We experience this static as tension and effort. Our lyrics become unintelligible and our sound dull or even pitchy. In contrast, when we target each vowel's pitch center, the frequencies produced by the harmonics and formants synchronize or "align", resulting with a beautiful tone.

As we know, the quality of the vowel sound is determined by the size and shape of **Containers 1** and **2**, which alter whenever we engage the muscles of the tongue, neck, jaw, soft palate, lips, and pharynx.[48] The larger the container, the darker the sound quality; the smaller the container, the brighter the sound quality.

Most vowels have four or more distinguishable formants, but **FORMANTS 1** and **2** determine a vowel's unique qualities and are what differentiate one vowel from another. **FORMANTS 1** and **2** are also the most "tunable" and for this reason, are referred to as **VOWEL AREA 1** and **VOWEL AREA 2**.[49] Depending on our tongue and mouth position, these formants will shift higher or lower in frequency.[50] This is important to remember as we make slight physical adjustments to find the "center" of each vowel.

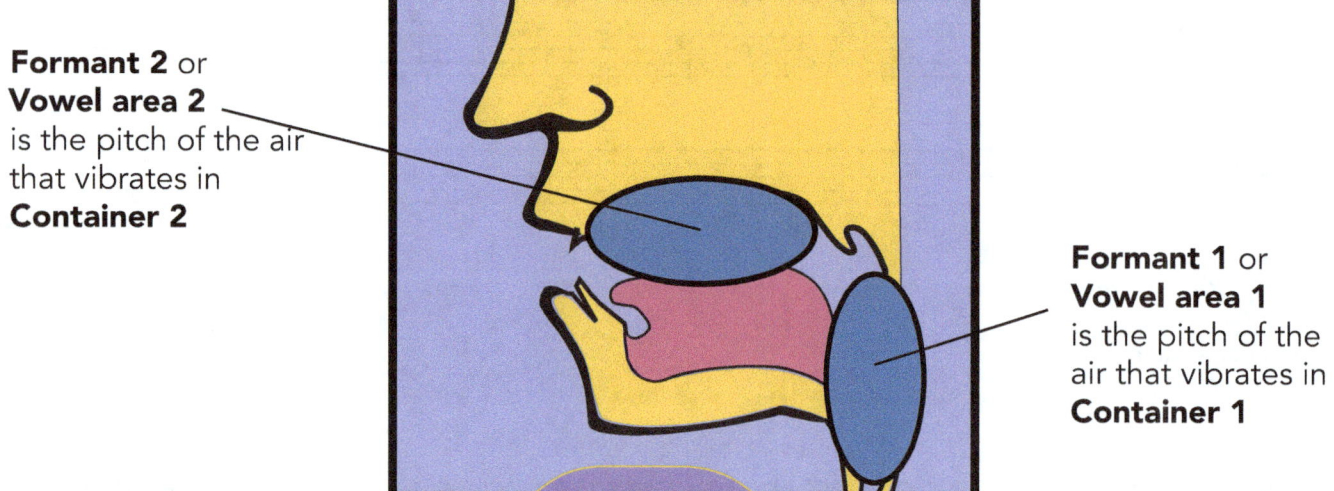

Formant 2 or **Vowel area 2** is the pitch of the air that vibrates in **Container 2**

Formant 1 or **Vowel area 1** is the pitch of the air that vibrates in **Container 1**

Once again, gently thump your fingernail against your larynx as you mouth all the vowels. What you are hearing is the **FORMANT 1** resonances for the vowels for *your* particular voice.[51] Open vowels, like [a], have high **FORMANT 1** frequencies while closed vowels like [i], have low **FORMANT 1** frequencies.

FORMANT 2 correlates to how forward or back the vowel is. Back vowels like [a], have low **FORMANT 2** frequencies while forward vowels like [i], have high **FORMANT 2** frequencies. Let's compare how **FORMANTS 1** and **2** shape the [a] and [i] vowels.

    [a] HOD

        * The jaw drops and the tongue is positioned back in the mouth.
- **Container 1** gets smaller.
- The pitch of **Formant 1** gets higher.
- **Container 2** gets larger.
- The pitch of **Formant 2** gets lower.

[i] HEED

* The highest part of the tongue comes forward and up.
    - **Container 1** gets larger.
    - The pitch of **Formant 1** gets lower.
    - **Container 2** gets smaller.
    - The pitch of **Formant 2** gets higher.

We must also consider the consonants preceding a vowel and following a vowel and how they affect the shape of our vocal tract, and therefore, the quality of the vowel.

* Try speaking the following words: **WITH, BILL, TIN**
    - Notice how the different consonants change the sounds of the **[I]** vowel.

The last point I would like to make is that as "sculptors of sound", we may bend some rules to achieve the sound we desire. However, it is important to understand the rules we are bending or even breaking! I suggest you always start from the "center" of the vowel, where the vowel is the purest and most efficient. Keep in mind that different musical genres approach vowels differently. What is acceptable when singing classical music might sound odd when singing jazz or contemporary musical theater.

Practice slowly and with intention. When working with lyrics, begin by eliminating all consonants. Focus on singing the vowels. When you think you have achieved the desired sound, add the consonants. If the consonants affect your resonance negatively, go back to singing the vowels and analyze how the consonants have altered your vocal tract. Try to maintain a consistent quality of sound by playing with **CONTAINER 1** and **CONTAINER 2** throughout your musical phrase. Your ear will guide you to make any necessary physical adjustments.

VOWEL EXERCISES

Choose one or two of the following activities for your daily practice.

Activity #41 VOWELS
* Sing [i] [e] [a] [o] [u] slowly, blending one vowel sound into another.
* Keep the tip of your tongue in contact with the bottom teeth while allowing the root of your tongue freedom to change position.

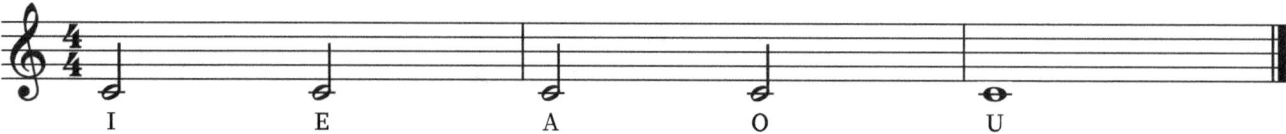

I E A O U

Activity #42 MI ME MA MO MU
* Use the /M/ to help target the "bounce-back" area.

Mi me ma mo mi me ma mo mi me ma mo mu

Activity #43 MOVING VOWELS
* Look for the "center" of each vowel.

I E A O U_____   I E A O U_____

Activity #44 BOUNCY VOWELS
This exercise requires a coordinated onset, as well as a stable vocal tract.

* Keep the tip of your tongue in contact with your bottom teeth while allowing the root of your tongue freedom to change position.
* Use ENERGY, DEPTH, & SPACE!

I E A O U   I E A O U   I E A O U   I E A O U

Activity #45 NI SLIDES
* Keep your larynx and vocal tract stable.

Activity #46 MEOW
* Exaggerate the "YOW" and feel a chewy stretch.
* Maintain a relaxed tongue.

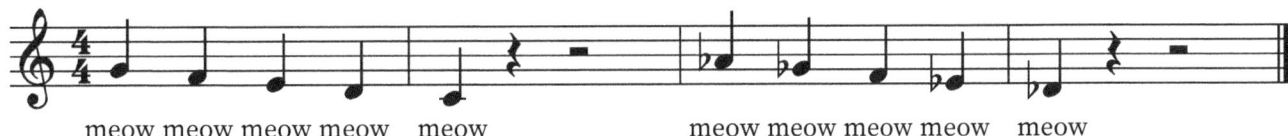

Activity #47 ME-YO
* Find the center of each vowel sound.

Activity #48 VE VI
* Keep your tongue lazy and fat!
  - Watch out for diphthongs!

Activity #49 CONSONANT TO VOWEL
* Use the consonant to "bounce" into the vowel.

Activity #50 OH, MY!
  * Watch out for diphthongs!

Oh ___ my _ Me _ oh _ my ___

Activity #51 KICK-OUT LIFTS!
We have had this exercise in **CHAPTER THREE - BREATH SUPPORT**, but now we are using it to "tune" our vowels and find their center.

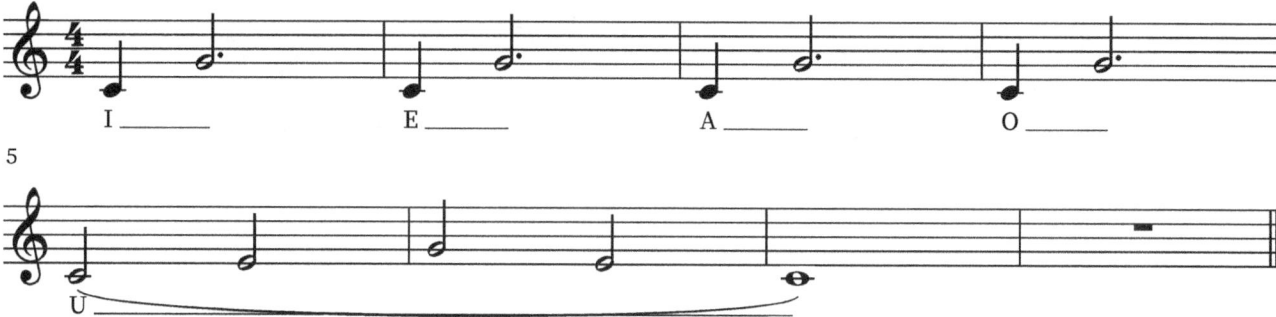

Activity # 52 DARK vs BRIGHT
  * Round your lips as you sing "no".
    - Your lips have extended your vocal tract.
    - Notice the darker tone quality.
  * Widen your lips as you sing "yea".
    - Your lips have shortened your vocal tract.
    - Notice the bright quality by.

No, no, no, no, yea, yea, yea, yea, yea

Activity #53 LAUGHING THE VOWELS
  * Bounce your epigastrium.
  * Keep a light staccato as you sing.

Hi Hi Hi Hi Hi Hi Hi He He He He He He He He Ha Ha Ha Ha Ho Ho Ho Ho Hu

Record your own exercises here.

RESONANCE EXERCISES SUMMARY

VOCAL TRACT:

1. TONGUE MASSAGE	p.70
2. HOLD OUR TONGUE	p.70
3. LITERALLY, HOLD YOUR TONGUE	p.70
4. TONGUE PRESSES	p.70
5. MOVE YOUR HEAD	p.70
6. JAW STRETCH	p.70
7. NECK STRETCH	p.70
8. OPEN THE BOX	p.71
9. SING WITH YOUR TONGUE OUT	p.71
10. TONGUE TWISTERS	p.71
11. ONE NOTE HUM	p.72
12. HEY-YA!	p.72
13. TONGUE INDEPENDENCE	p.72
14. YUM-YUM	p.72
15. NG-AH	p.73
16. MAY-A	p.73
17. SU-LU	p.73
18. DUH!	p.73
19. KANA	p.74
20. TONGUE RELEASE	p.74
21. LI-LO	p.74
22. RED LEATHER	p.74
23. LA-GA	p.75
24. LOUIE!	p.75
25. "K" STUTTER	p.75
26. BOI	p.75
27. KITTELY KIT	p.76
28. BI-GI-DI	p.76
29. LAZY BABY	p.76
30. MA-OH	p.77
31. MELLOW	p.77

SEMI-OCCLUDED VOCAL TRACT (SOVT)

    32. SIRENS   p.81
    33. LIP TRILLS   p.81
    34. STRAW BUBBLES   p.81
    35. STRAW VOWELS   p.81
    36. SING A SONG   p.82
    37. VIBRATE THE ARTICULATORS p.82
    38. OCTAVES PLUS   p.82
    39. SLOPPY DUCK   p.82
    40. NG SLIDES   p.82

VOWELS

    41. VOWELS   p.90
    42. MI ME MA MO MU   p.90
    43. MOVING VOWELS   p.90
    44. BOUNCY VOWELS   p.90
    45. NI SLIDES   p.91
    46. MEOW   p.91
    47. ME-YO   p.91
    48. VE-VI   p.91
    49. CONSONANT - VOWEL   p.91
    50. OH, MY!   p.92
    51. KICK-OUT LIFTS   p.92
    52. DARK vs BRIGHT   p.92
    53. LAUGHING THE VOWELS   p.92

RESONANCE REVIEW QUESTIONS

1. What is the main resonator for the human voice?
　* The vocal tract.

2. What is another name for the throat?
　* The pharynx.

3. What are the three parts of the Pharynx?
　* The naso-pharynx, the oro-pharynx, and the laryngo-pharynx.

4. What are the two big actions that can change the shape of the pharynx or throat?
　* Swallowing and yawning.

5. What "balance" of resonance are we looking for when we sing?
　* Nasal and laryngeal.

6. Why is straw phonation a healthy way to warm up?
　* Because there is an increase of back pressure which makes it difficult to compress and squeeze our larynx. The air from our lungs and the air reflected back at the lips are both vibrating our vocal folds.

7. Name two areas the root of the tongue attaches to.
　* The larynx (specifically the hyoid bone) and the jaw.

8. What is the ideal position of the tongue?
　* Cradled in the jaw and in contact with the lower teeth.

9. What are some common jaw issues?
　* Thrusting the jaw forward and compressing our larynx to avoid the break.

10. What's the easiest way to relieve jaw tension?
　* Massage and awareness.

11. Where is the soft palate located?
　* The spongy area of the roof of the mouth towards the back of the throat.

12. What is the ideal shape for the soft palate?
　* The beginning of an 'internal' smile.

13. What happens if we lift the soft palate into a full yawn?
　* It can shut off the nasopharynx from the rest of the pharynx and result in a muted sound. Lifting the soft palate also lowers the larynx and can introduce tension.

14. What are the colors correlating to each vowel sound in singing?
   * green, beige, aqua, gold, blue.

15. Name the 5 main articulators
   * The jaw, the tongue, the teeth, the lips, and the soft palate.

TROUBLESHOOTING

CHAPTER 7 - VOCAL TRACT

1. Is your tongue remaining in contact with the lower teeth as you sing? Is your tongue tensing at the root?
 * Try any of the tongue release exercises.

2. Do you grind your teeth? Bite the inside of your mouth? Chew a lot of gum?
 * Work on eliminating negative daily habits.

3. Are you holding your soft palate in a "yawn" position?
 * Lifting the soft palate can block the nasal passages and result in a muted sound.

4. Are you lowering or flattening your soft palate
 * Think of something humorous and make a small smile from top molar to top molar inside your mouth.

5. Do you understand how your vocal tract functions?
 * Think of your vocal tract as a paper towel tube. Take turns placing your fingers on your larynx, throat, and face as you hum. Feel the vibration move around as you change pitch.

CHAPTER 8 - SOVT (SEMI-OCCLUDED VOCAL TRACT)

1. Do you think you are working too hard to sing?
 * Practice with any of the SOVT exercises.

CHAPTER 9 - VOWELS

1. Does your tone sound sharp or flat even though you a e on the pitch?
 * Make sure your vowels are "centered".

2. Is it difficult to understand your lyrics
 * Check you are not modifying your vowels too much.

RESONANCE

RESONANCE

Can You Hear Me Now?

What an accomplishment! You have completed the final section on **RESONANCE**, and now understand what makes your voice uniquely yours!

* We have explored how our articulators affect our vocal tract.
* We have discovered a valuable tool, the straw, and how SOVT exercises allow us to explore the parameters of our vocal range safely.
* We have learned about vowels, vowel modification, harmonics, and formants.
* Finally, we recognize how small physical changes to our vocal tract affect our sound.

Well done! Now it's time to put it all together and use the three fundamental foundations: **ENERGY, VIBRATION,** and **RESONANCE** to explore your voice and make new discoveries. The relationships between energy, vibration, and resonance are never static. Explore how each element affects one another and our instrument as a whole.

In this book, we have focused solely on technique. You have "built" your instrument. Now let your technique serve your limitless creative expression. As singers, we are storytellers capable of expressing every human emotion. Let the lyrics guide you. Enjoy the journey! Keep singing! The possibilities are within you waiting to be revealed.

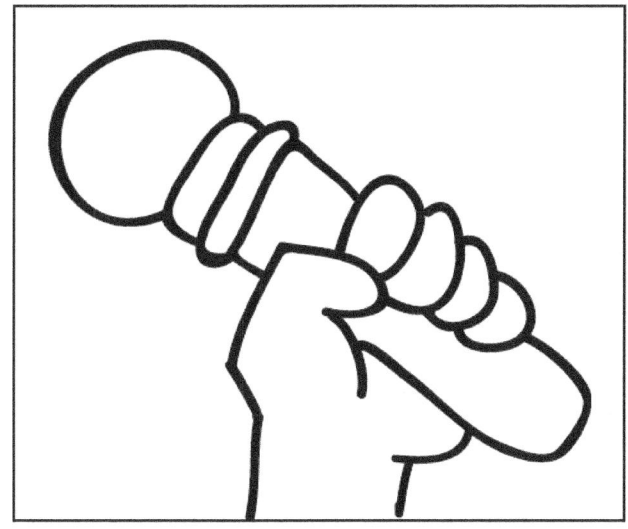

SAMPLE WARM-UPS

Use the following sample warm-ups to get started. As you build your own warm-ups, take a few exercises from each area; ENERGY, VIBRATION, and RESONANCE.

#1

ENERGY
* Body Stretch (p.8)
* Diaphragm awareness (p.13)
* Less is More (p.21)
* Hush! (p.21)

VIBRATION
* Puppy Whimpers (p.40)
* Counting 1,2,3 (p.40)
* Sirens (p.50)

RESONANCE
* Tongue massage (p.70)
* Jaw stretch (p.70)
* One note hum (p.72)
* Straw sirens! (p.81)
* Vowels (p.90)

#2

ENERGY
* Roll down (p.8)
* Smell the bread (p.13)
* 8-8-16 (p.15)
* Quiet, please! (p.21)

VIBRATION
* Move our Head (p.40)
* The sneeze (p.46)
* Hip (p.50)

RESONANCE
* Hold your tongue (p.70)
* Hey-ya (p.72)
* Lip trills (p.81)
* Mi me ma mo mu (p.90)

#3

🟩 ENERGY
- * Line it up (p.8)
- * Back breathing (p.13)
- * Inflate a balloon (p.21)

🟨 VIBRATION
- * Connect the cords (p.40)
- * Talk like a mouse (p.46)
- * Hey, Taxi! (p.50)

🟦 RESONANCE
- * Literally, hold your tongue (p.70)
- * Yum-yum (p.72)
- * Straw bubbles (p.81)
- * Moving vowels (p.90)

#4

🟩 ENERGY
- * Descriptive Words (p. 8)
- * Suspend the breath (p.14)
- * Lift the piano (p.22)

🟨 VIBRATION
- * Find it! (p.40)
- * Cop Car! (p.46)
- * Mom! (p.51)

🟦 RESONANCE
- * Tongue Presses (p.70)
- * Ng-ah (p.73)
- * Straw vowels (p.81)
- * Bouncy Vowels (p.90)

#5

▮ ENERGY
- Roll down (p.8)
- Intercostal stretches (p.16)
- Book on belly (p.23)

▮ VIBRATION
- No more secrets (p.41)
- Cop car! (p.46)
- The Tease (p.51)

▮ RESONANCE
- Neck stretch (p.70)
- May-a (p.73)
- Vibrate the articulators (p.82)
- Kick-out lifts (p.92)

#6

▮ ENERGY
- Body stretch (p.8)
- YWTL (p.9)
- Squat breaths (p.16)
- Kick-out lifts (p.24)

▮ VIBRATION
- Puppy Whimpers (p.40)
- The duck (p.51)
- Sloppy duck (p.52)
- Morning Brings (p.52)

▮ RESONANCE
- Tongue presses (p.70)
- Open the box (p.71)
- Louie (p.75)
- Octave plus (p.82)
- Me-yo (p.91)

#7

🟩 ENERGY
* YTWL (p.9)
* Neck Rolls (p.9)
* Pull the string (p.14)
* Shake hands (p.23)

🟨 VIBRATION
* Find It! (p.34)
* Hip (p.50)
* Mom! (p.51)

🟦 RESONANCE
* Straw sirens (p.81)
* Lip trills (p.81)
* Bouncy Vowels (p.90)
* Dark vs Bright (p.92)

#8

🟩 ENERGY
* Line it up (p.8)
* Suspend the breath (p.14)
* Kick-out lifts (p.24)

🟨 VIBRATION
* Puppy whimpers (p.40)
* Sigh (p.50)
* Lighten up (p.51)

🟦 RESONANCE
* Yum-yum (p.72)
* Ma-oh (p.77)
* Ng slides (p.82)
* Ni slides (.91)

#9

■ ENERGY
   * Line it up (p.8)
   * Squat breaths (p.16)
   * Book on belly (p. 23)
   * Kick-out lifts (p.24)

■ VIBRATION
   * Find it! (p.40)
   * Puppy whimpers (p.40)
   * Hip (p.50)

■ RESONANCE
   * Vowels (p.90)
   * "K" stutter (p.75)
   * Kick-out lifts (p.92)

#10

■ ENERGY
   * Descriptive words (p. 8)
   * Fill the vacuum (p.15)
   * Planks and belts (p.22)

■ VIBRATION
   * Move your head (p.40)
   * Hip (p.50)
   * Sloppy Duck (p.52)
   * Morning Brings (p.52)

■ RESONANCE
   * Tongue massage (p.70)
   * Jaw stretch (p.70)
   * Li-lo (p.74)
   * Kick-out lifts (p.92)

BIBLIOGRAPHY

1 Adapted from Melissa Malde, MaryJean Allen, and Kurt-Alexander Zeller, *What Every Singer Needs To Know About Their Body* (San Diego, Oxford, Brisbane: Plural Publishing, Inc., 2009), 11

2 Ibid.,16

3 Ibid., 16

4 Ibid., 27

5 Ibid., 16

6 Ibid., 19

7 Ibid., 12

8 Ibid., 12

9 Ibid., 66-67

10 Adapted from James C. McKinney, *The Diagnosis & Correction of Vocal Faults: A Manual for Teachers of Singing & Choir Directors* (Long Grove: Waveland Press, Inc., 1994), 48

11 Adapted from Kristin Linklater, *Freeing the Natural Voice: Imagery and Art in the Practice of Voice and Language* (Hollywood: Drama Publishers, 2006), 225-226

12 Adapted from James Nestor, *Breath: The New Science of a Lost Art* (New York: Riverhead Books, 2020), 219-230

13 Adapted from Graham Hewitt, *How to Sing* (New York: Taplinger Publishing Co., Inc., 1978), 5

14 Adapted from Per Bristow, *Sing With Freedom* (The Singing Zone, accessed March 11, 2021), www.TheSingingZone.com

15 Adapted from Laurel Irene and David Harris, *Voice Science Works* (voicescienceworks.org/breath.html, accessed March, 2021), https://www.voicescienceworks.org

16 Adapted from Malde, Allen, Zeller, *What Every Singer Needs To Know About Their Body*, 77

17 Ibid., 69

18 Ibid., 69

19 Adapted from Laurel Irene and David Harris, https://www.voicescienceworks.org/appoggio.html

20 Adapted from Malde, Allen, Zeller, *What Every Singer Needs To Know About Their Body*, 69

21 Adapted from Cheryl Porter, *Cheryl Porter Vocal Method* (https://course.cherylportermethod.com/, accessed April, 2021), https://cherylportermethod.com/

22 Ibid., https://cherylportermethod.com/

23 Adapted from Malde, Allen, Zeller, *What Every Singer Needs To Know About Their Body*, 27-28

24 Ibid., 101

25 Adapted from https://www.singwise.com/articles/vowels-formants-modifications

26 Adapted from Adapted from Hewitt, *How to Sing*, 14

27 Adapted from Manuel Garcia, *Hints on Singing*, (New York: Shuberth & Co., 1894), 7

28 Adapted from Malde, Allen, Zeller, *What Every Singer Needs To Know About Their Body*, 99

29 Adapted from Scott McCoy, *Your Voice: An Inside View, Second Edition.* Copyright, 2012, 18

30 Adapted from McKinney, *The Diagnosis & Correction of Vocal Faults: A Manual for Teachers of Singing & Choir Directors*, 182-185

31 Ibid., p.93

32 Adapted from Manuel Garcia, *Hints on Singing*, (New York: Shuberth & Co., 1894), 7

33 Adapted from McKinney, *The Diagnosis & Correction of Vocal Faults: A Manual for Teachers of Singing & Choir Directors*, 182-184

34 Ibid., 182

35 Ibid., 184

36 Adapted from Kenneth H. Phillips, *Teaching Kids to Sing*, (New York: Schirmer Books, 1996), 296

37 Adapted from Irene and Harris, https://www.voicescienceworks.org/vocal-tract.html

38 Ibid, https://www.voicescienceworks.org/vocal-tract.html

39 Adapted from Linklater, *Freeing the Natural Voice: Imagery and Art in the Practice of Voice and Language*, 142

40 Ibid., 310

41 Adapted from Hewitt, *How to Sing*, 17

42 Adapted from Irene and Harris, https://www.voicescienceworks.org/sovt-exercises.html

43 Adapted from Irene and Harris, https://voicestraw.com/pages/the-science

44 Ibid., https://voicestraw.com/pages/the-science

45 Adapted from Kenneth H. Phillips, *Teaching Kids to Sing*, (New York: Schirmer Books, 1996), 277

46 Adapted from Kenneth W. Bozeman, *Kinesthetic Voice Pedagogy 2: Motivating Acoustic Efficiency*, (Gahanna: Inside View Press, 2021), 40

47 Adapted from https://www.singwise.com/articles/vowels-formants-modifications

48 Adapted from Irene and Harris, https://www.voicescienceworks.org/harmonics-vs-formants.html

49 Ibid., https://www.voicescienceworks.org/harmonics-vs-formants.html

50 Adapted from https://www.singwise.com/articles/vowels-formants-modifications

51 Ibid., //www.singwise.com/articles/vowels-formants-modifications

References

Bristow, Per. *Sing With Freedom.* www.TheSingingZone.com
Garcia, Manuel, *Hints on Singing.* Copyright, 1894
Hewitt, Graham. *How to Sing.* Copyright, 1978
Irene, L., Harris, D., *Voice Science Works.* www.voicescienceworks.org
Linklater, Kristin. *Freeing the Natural Voice.* Copyright, 2006
Malde, M., Allen, M., Zeller, K-A., *What Every Singer Needs to Know About the Body.* Copyright, 2009
McCoy, Scott. *Your Voice: An Inside View, Second Edition.* Copyright, 2012
McKinney, James C. *The Diagnosis and Correction of Vocal Faults.* Copyright, 1994
Nestor, James. *Breath.* Copyright, 2020
O'Connor, Karyn. *SingWise.* https://www.singwise.com
Phillips, Kenneth H. *Teaching Kids to Sing.* Copyright, 1996
Porter, Cheryl. *Cheryl Porter Vocal Method.* https://cherylportermethod.com
Titze, Ingo. https://www.youtube.com/watch?v=asDg7T-WT-0

Additional Suggested Reading

Cooper, Dr. Morton. *Change Your Voice, Change Your Life.* Copyright, 1984

Index

A

Abdominal muscles, 18, 24
    internal oblique muscles, 19
    external oblique muscles, 19
    transverse abdominal, 19
    rectus abdominis, 19
Acoustics, 87
    frequency, 43, 87
    formants, 87-89
    formant one, 88-89
    formant two, 88-89
    fundamental frequency, 87
    harmonics, 87
    overtone series, 87
Alignment, body, 5
Articulators, 65-69
Arytenoid cartilage 44
Atlas-Occipital joint, 5-6, 8
Attack *(see phonation, onset)*

B

Balanced onset, *(see phonation)*
Body alignment, 5
"Break", 47, 79
Breath, 1, 11-16
Breath support, 17-25
    core, 19
    muscles of, 18-20
Breathy onset *(see phonation)*
Bright quality, 64

C

Chest voice *(see Registers and Register coordination)*
Clavicular breathing, 18
Container One, 64, 65, 87
Container Two, 64-65, 88-89
Core, 19
Coordinated onset, *(see phonation)*
Cricothyroid ligament, *(see Registers)*

D

Diaphragm muscle, 11-12, 13, 19, 20
Diphthongs, 84
Dark quality, 64

E
    Energy, 1-33
        introduction, 1
    "Energy, Depth and Space", 47-49
    Epigastrium, 20
    External oblique muscles, 19

F
    Formants, *(see Acoustics)*
    Frequency, 43, 87
    Fundamental frequency, 87

G
    Glottis, 17, 37, 40

H
    Harmonic-overtone series, 87
    Hyoid bone, 44, 66

I
    Inner abdominal canister, 19, 20
        pelvic floor, 20
    Intercostal muscles, 12, 16
        internal intercostals, 12
        external intercostals, 12

J
    Jaw, 67

K
    "Kick-out" area, 19, 20, 24

L
    Larynx, 17, 18
    Lips, 69
    Lumbar spine, 5-7

M
    Monophthongs, 83
    Mouth cavity, 64

N
    Nodules, 39

O
    Onset, *(see phonation)*
    Overtone series *(see acoustics)*

P
    Pelvic floor, 20
    Pharynx, 64, 65
        laryngopharynx, 65
        oropharynx, 65
        nasopharynx, 65

Phonation, 37-41
    breathy onset, 38
    coordinated or balanced onset, 37, 38
    glottal onset 38
Polyps, 39
Posture, 5-9

R

Registers, 43-46, 47-48
    "chest" voice, 43, 44, 47, 48
    cricothyroid ligament (CT ligament), 44, 45, 47
    depth and, 48
    energy and, 40
    falsetto, 43
    "head" voice, 43, 44, 47, 48
    "middle" voice, 43, 44, 47, 48
    modal register, 43
    space and, 47-49
    thyroarytenoid ligament (TA ligament), 44, 45, 47
    vocal fry register, 43
    vocal registration *(see Register coordination)*
    whistle register, 43
    register coordination, 47- 52
    vocal break, 47, 79
    vocal registration, 39
Resonance, 1, 49, 61-101

S

Semi-occluded vocal tract, 79-82
SOVT *(see semi-occluded vocal tract)*
Soft palate, 63, 68
Spine, *(see posture)*
Sound waves, 37, 63, 64
Subglottic pressure, 18, 20, 37

T

Thyroid cartilage, 44
Thyroarytenoid ligament *(See Registers)*
Tongue, 66
Trachea, 18

V

Vocal tract, 1, 63-77
Vowels, 83-92
Vowel resonance, 84-86
Vowel modification, 86
Vibration, 1, 35-59
Vocal folds, 17, 20, 37, 39, 43-45

Acknowledgments

This book is a labor of love, springing from decades of teaching hundreds of students. Every lesson was an opportunity for me to further explore the amazing HUMAN VOICE. To all of my students, past and present, thank you for trusting and humoring me with my sometimes unusual exercises and for returning time and time again!

A special thank you to Charlotte Finelli, my cherished friend, editor, and confidant. To Jupiter Dune, Gabrielle Fox, Luke Weber, Michael Patrick Sullivan, Shaunna Spinks, and Shammara Lawrence, for keeping me accountable every week and reminding me to have fun! To Avis Larson, for not only being an amazing sister, but for all of your help with the cover. You have an uncanny knack for saving the day! To my very talented mother, Lorraine Moseley Epstein, for a lifetime of love and encouragement. To my wonderful family, Graham, Max, Oliver, and Charlie, for graciously sharing our home with countless students and their families over the years. Thank you all for patiently reading multiple versions of this book and for your invaluable input. I am so grateful and love you all.

Visit **www.anngulianvocalstudio.com** to access the accompanying recordings for all exercises.

Password Code: **Ha8W76ja49**

www.ingramcontent.com/pod-product-compliance
Lightning Source LLC
Chambersburg PA
CBHW080552230426
43663CB00015B/2812